TEACHER'S PET PUBLICATIONS

LITPLAN TEACHER PACK
for
The Watsons Go to Birmingham – 1963
based on the book by
Christopher Paul Curtis

Written by
Barbara M. Linde, MA Ed.

© 2006 Teacher's Pet Publications
All Rights Reserved

The Lit Plan on *The Watsons Go to Birmingham* has been brought to you
by Teacher's Pet Publications, Inc.

Copyright Teacher's Pet Publications 2006
All Rights Reserved
11504 Hammock Point
Berlin, MD 21811

Only the student materials in this unit plan may be reproduced.
Pages such as worksheets and study guides may be reproduced
only for use in the purchaser's classroom.

For any additional copyright questions, contact Teacher's Pet Publications.

www.tpet.com

TABLE OF CONTENTS *The Watsons Go to Birmingham*

Introduction	7
Unit Objectives	10
Reading Assignment Sheet	11
Unit Outline	12
Study Questions	15
Quiz/Study Questions (Multiple Choice)	26
Pre-Reading Vocabulary Worksheets	45
Lesson One (Introductory Lesson)	65
Nonfiction Assignment Sheet	68
Oral Reading Evaluation Form	71
Writing Assignment 1	75
Writing Evaluation Form	76
Writing Assignment 2	82
Extra Writing Assignments/ Discussion Questions	87
Quotations	89
Writing Assignment 3	93
Vocabulary Review Activities	94
Unit Review Activities	96
Unit Tests	103
Unit Resource Materials	147
Vocabulary Resource Materials	165

A FEW NOTES ABOUT THE AUTHOR
Christopher Paul Curtis

Christopher Paul Curtis was born and raised in Flint, Michigan (the setting for *Bud, Not Buddy* and *The Watsons Go to Birmingham-1963)*. After graduating from school, he worked on the assembly line of the Fisher Body Flint Plant 1 until his wife suggested that he "better hurry up and start doing something constructive" with his life, at which time be began his writing career. Mr. Curtis attended the University of Michigan and won the Avery Hopwood Prize as well as the Jules Hopwood Prize for some of his writing there. Mr. Curtis's major publications include *The Watsons go To Birmingham - 1963* (Newberry Honor and Coretta Scott King Honor) and *Bud, Not Buddy* (Newberry Medal, Coretta Scott King Award). Windsor, Ontario, Canada is his current home, where he lives with his wife Kaysandra and children Steven Darrell and Cydney McKenzie. His real-life grandfathers were Earl "Lefty" Lewis, a Negro Baseball League pitcher, and Herman E. Curtis, Sr., a 1930's bandleader of "Herman Curtis and the Dusky Devastators of the Depression."

INTRODUCTION *The Watsons Go to Birmingham–1963*

This unit has been designed to develop students' reading, writing, thinking, listening, and speaking skills through exercises and activities related to *The Watsons Go to Birmingham–1963* by Christopher Paul Curtis. It includes 20 lessons, supported by extra resource materials.

The **introductory lesson** introduces students to the story. Following the introductory activity, students are given an explanation of how the activity relates to the book they are about to read. Following the transition, students are given the materials they will be using during the unit. They are also introduced to the nonfiction assignment.

The **reading assignments** are approximately 30 pages each; some are a little shorter while others are a little longer. Students have approximately 15 minutes of pre-reading work to do prior to each reading assignment. This pre-reading work involves reviewing the study questions for the assignment and doing some vocabulary work for 6 to 10 vocabulary words they will encounter in their reading.

The **study guide questions** are fact-based questions; students can find the answers to these questions right in the text. These questions come in two formats: short answer or multiple choice. The best use of these materials is probably to use the short answer version of the questions as study guides for students (since answers will be more complete), and to use the multiple-choice version for occasional quizzes. It might be a good idea to make transparencies of your answer keys for the overhead projector.

The **vocabulary work** is intended to enrich students' vocabularies as well as to aid in the students' understanding of the book. Prior to each reading assignment, students will complete a two-part worksheet for approximately 6 to 10 vocabulary words in the upcoming reading assignment. Part I focuses on students' use of general knowledge and contextual clues by giving the sentence in which the word appears in the text. Students are then to write down what they think the words mean based on the words' usage. Part II gives students dictionary definitions of the words and has them match the words to the correct definitions based on the words' contextual usage. Students should then have an understanding of the words when they meet them in the text.

After each reading assignment, students will go back and formulate answers for the study guide questions. Discussion of these questions serves as a review of the most important events and ideas presented in the reading assignments.

After students complete extra discussion questions, there is a vocabulary review lesson which pulls together all of the separate vocabulary lists for the reading assignments and gives students a review of all of the words they have studied.

Following the reading of the book, a lesson is devoted to the extra discussion questions/writing assignments. These questions focus on interpretation, critical analysis and personal response, employing a variety of thinking skills and adding to the students' understanding of the novel. These questions are done as a **group activity**.

Using the information they have acquired so far through individual work and class discussions, students get together to further examine the text and to brainstorm ideas relating to the themes of the novel.

The group activity is followed by a **reports and discussion** session in which the groups share their ideas about the book with the entire class; thus, the entire class gets exposed to many different ideas regarding the themes and events of the book.

There are **three writing assignments** in this unit, each with the purpose of informing, persuading, or expressing personal opinions. The first assignment is to **persuade**. Students will take the role of Kenny and persuade Byron to improve his behavior. The second writing assignment is to **inform**. Students will create a notebook like Momma's to plan for a trip. The third writing assignment is to **express personal opinions**. Students will respond to a statement that Kenny says in the last chapter of the book.

In addition, there is a **nonfiction reading assignment**. Students are required to read a piece of nonfiction related in some way to *The Watsons Go to Birmingham–1963*. After reading their nonfiction pieces, students will fill out a worksheet on which they answer questions regarding facts, interpretation, criticism, and personal opinions. During one class period, students make oral presentations about the nonfiction pieces they have read. This not only exposes all students to a wealth of information; it also gives students the opportunity to practice public speaking.

The **review lesson** pulls together all of the aspects of the unit. The teacher is given four or five choices of activities or games to use which all serve the same basic function of reviewing all of the information presented in the unit.

There are five different unit tests included. Two are multiple choice, two are short answer and there is also an advanced short answer unit test.

There are additional **support materials** included with this unit. The **resource materials sections** include suggestions for an in-class library, crossword and word search puzzles related to the novel, and extra vocabulary worksheets. There is a list of **bulletin board ideas** which gives the teacher suggestions for bulletin boards to go along with this unit. In addition, there is a list of extra class activities the teacher could choose from to enhance the unit or as a substitution for an exercise the teacher might feel is inappropriate for his/her class. Answer keys are located directly after the reproducible student materials throughout the unit.

UNIT PLAN ADAPTATIONS – *The Watsons Go to Birmingham–1963*

Block Schedule

Depending on the length of your class periods, and the frequency with which the class meets, you may wish to choose one of the following options:
- Complete two of the daily lessons in one class period.
- Have students complete all reading and writing activities in class.
- Assign all reading to be completed out of class, and concentrate on the worksheets and discussions in class.
- Assign the projects from the daily lessons at the beginning of the unit, and allow time each day for students to work on them.
- Use some of the Unit and Vocabulary Resource activities during every class.

Gifted & Talented / Advanced Classes
- Emphasize the projects and the extra discussion questions.
- Have students complete all of the writing activities.
- Assign the reading to be completed out of class and focus on the discussions in class.
- Encourage students to develop their own questions.

ESL / ELD
- Assign a partner to help the student read the text aloud.
- Tape record the text and have the student listen and follow along in the text.
- Give the student the study guide worksheets to use as they read.
- Provide pictures and demonstrations to explain difficult vocabulary words and concepts.
- Conduct guided reading lessons, asking students to stop frequently and explain what they have read.
- Show the movie version of the novel and help students identify characters and events, and relate the action in their own words. You may want to show the movie without the sound and explain the actions in your own words.

UNIT OBJECTIVES – *The Watsons Go to Birmingham–1963*

1. Through reading *The Watsons Go to Birmingham* students will analyze characters and their situations to better understand the themes of the novel.

2. Students will identify the details in the setting that help them understand the time period in which the novel is set as well as the author's purpose for writing the story.

3. Students will demonstrate their understanding of the text on four levels: factual, interpretive, critical, and personal.

4. Students will be able to identify and discuss the moods in the novel and explain when and why the mood changes.

5. Students will practice reading aloud and silently to improve their skills in each area.

6. Students will enrich their vocabularies and improve their understanding of the novel through the vocabulary lessons prepared for use in conjunction with it.

7. Students will answer questions to demonstrate their knowledge and understanding of the main events and characters in *The Watsons Go to Birmingham–1963*.

8. Students will practice writing through a variety of writing assignments.

9. The writing assignments in this are geared to several purposes:
    a. To check the students' reading comprehension
    b. To make students think about the ideas presented by the novel
    c. To make students put those ideas into perspective
    d. To encourage critical and logical thinking
    e. To provide the opportunity to practice good grammar and improve students' use of the English language.

10. Students will read aloud, report, and participate in large and small group discussions to improve their public speaking and personal interaction skills.

READING ASSIGNMENT SHEET
The Watsons Go to Birmingham–1963

Date Assigned	Reading Assignment	Completion Date
	Chapters 1-2	
	Chapters 3-4	
	Chapters 5-6	
	Chapters 7-8	
	Chapters 9-10	
	Chapters 11-12	
	Chapters 13-14	
	Chapter 15	

WRITING ASSIGNMENT LOG
The Watsons Go to Birmingham–1963

Date Assigned	Writing Assignment	Completion Date
	Writing Assignment 1	
	Writing Assignment 2	
	Writing Assignment 3	
	Non-fiction Assignment	

UNIT OUTLINE *The Watsons Go to Birmingham–1963*

1	2	3	4	5
Introduction Nonfiction Assignment	PVR Chapters 1-2 Study ?? Chapters 1-2	PVR Chapters 3-4 Oral Reading Evaluation	Study ?? Chapters 3-4 Minilesson: Character Traits	PVR Study ?? Chapters 5-6 Writing Assignment #1
6	7	8	9	10
PVR Study ?? Chapters 7-8	Quiz Chapters 1-8 Writing Conference PVR Chapters 9-10	Study?? Chapters 9-10 Minilesson: Setting	Writing Assignment #2	PVR Chapters 11-12
11	12	13	14	15
Study?? Chapters 11-12 PVR Chapters 13-14	Study?? Chapters 13-14 PVR Chapter 15	Study?? Chapter 15 Minilesson: Mood	Extra Writing/Discussion Questions	Quotations Graphic Organizers
16	17	18	19	20
Writing Assignment #3	Vocabulary Review	Unit Review	Test	Nonfiction Assignment

Key: **P** = Preview Study Questions **V** = Vocabulary Work **R** = Read

STUDY GUIDE QUESTIONS

SHORT ANSWER STUDY GUIDE QUESTIONS
The Watsons Go to Birmingham–1963

Chapters 1-2
1. What did Momma call Michigan?
2. Where was Momma from originally?
3. What was Byron called since he turned age thirteen?
4. What did Momma do when she thought something was funny? Why did she do that?
5. What did Dad tell the family there was in downtown Birmingham?
6. What happened to Byron when he and Kenny were scraping the ice off the car windows?
7. What was Kenny's nickname for the family?
8. What did Kenny call Byron after the incident with the ice on the car windows? Why?
9. Whom did Kenny refer to as the king of grades K-4 and the god of the school?
10. Why did the other kids tease Kenny? What did Byron tell him to do about it?
11. How did Kenny think of Rufus and why?
12. What did the family call the car? What kind of car was it?

Chapters 3-4
1. What did Kenny think would happen when the teacher sat Rufus next to him in class? Was he right or wrong? Explain what happened.
2. What did Kenny find out about Rufus and his brother Cody?
3. Why had Kenny stopped playing with LJ Jones?
4. Why didn't Kenny mind playing with Rufus?
5. Why was Rufus upset with Kenny? What happened as a result? How did Kenny feel? How was the problem solved?
6. Why did Momma make the children wear so many clothes in the winter?
7. What was Byron's explanation for why they had to wear so many clothes? How did this explanation affect Joey?
8. Describe the game called "The Great Carp Escape." Explain who was playing it and why. Tell how Kenny felt about the game.

Chapters 5-6
1. What did Momma catch Byron doing and what did she say she would do to him?
2. Was Momma successful in carrying out her threat? Explain why or why not.
3. What did Momma tell the boys to do when they went to Mitchell's store for some groceries? What did Byron think this meant, and how did he feel about it? Was Byron's assumption correct?
4. What did Byron do after he found out the truth about the list at Mitchell's store?
5. Describe what happened to the mourning dove.

Short Answer Study Guide Questions *The Watsons Go to Birmingham–1963*

Chapters 7-8
1. What did Byron do to his hair? What did Momma say about it? What was Byron's reason for doing it?
2. What did Dad do about Byron's hair? What song did he whistle during the process?
3. What did Dad tell Byron after the punishment had been completed?
4. Who is Grandma Sands?
5. Kenny described his parents as acting strange after they talked to Grandma Sands. What were they doing?
6. Dad bought something very special for the car that he asked Joey to put on the car. What was it and how did Dad describe it?
7. There was something in the Watson house that Dad did not keep with the ones that belonged to the rest of the family. What was it, and why did Dad keep his separate?
8. What did Dad put in the car? How did Momma react when she saw it? What did the children think?
9. What was Momma's song? What was Kenny's song?
10. What news did the parents tell the children while they were all sitting in the car listening to the records? What were their reasons for this news?

Chapters 9-10
1. Dad talked with Kenny about the reasons they were sending Byron to Alabama. What did Dad tell Kenny?
2. How did Kenny feel when Dad talked to him like a grown-up?
3. Summarize the incident when Mrs. Davidson gave a gift to Joey.
4. Where did Byron have to sleep the night before the family left on the trip, and why?
5. On the trip, Kenny asked why they could not drive until Dad was tired and then stop for the day. What was Dad's reply? How did he sound when he answered?
6. What was the title of Momma's notebook? What was on the cover? What were the contents?
7. How did Byron plan to pay his parents back for making him go to Alabama? Was he successful?
8. Dad planned ahead of time to do something on the trip but not tell Momma. What was it?
9. Kenny described something on their trip as the scariest things he had ever seen. What were they? Why did he think these things were scary?
10. How did Dad describe driving through the mountains?

Short Answer Study Guide Questions *The Watsons Go to Birmingham–1963*

Chapters 11-12
1. What made Kenny think that Dad was very tired?
2. Kenny thought that Birmingham looked a lot like another place. What place was that? What surprised Kenny about Birmingham?
3. What did Kenny expect Grandma Sands to look like? What did she really look like?
4. What fictional characters did Kenny use to describe how he expected the meeting between Grandma Sands and Byron to go? What characters did he use to describe how the meeting actually went? How did Kenny feel about the reality of the meeting?
5. How did Kenny describe Birmingham?
6. Who was Mr. Robert?
7. What took the children a while to get used to?
8. What did Kenny think about making Byron spend a whole summer in the heat? How did Byron seem to be taking it?

Chapters 13-14
1. What place were the children told to stay away from and why?
2. How did Byron describe the whirlpool?
3. Where did Kenny go? Did Byron and Joey go with him?
4. Describe what happened to Kenny when he went in the water.
5. What did Byron do when Kenny was out of the water?
6. What was the noise that Kenny and the others heard?
7. Describe what Kenny did and saw when he got to the church.
8. Describe the conversation between Joey and Kenny back at Grandma Sands's house.
9. What did Joey tell Kenny about her time in the church that morning?
10. What did Kenny realize when Grandma Sands asked where his parents were? What did he do then?

Chapter 15
1. Who threw the bomb?
2. Who was killed and injured?
3. How did Kenny's parents take the bombing?
4. When and why did the family leave Birmingham?
5. Which one of the children were the parents the most worried about? Why?
6. Where was Kenny going when he disappeared?
7. What did Byron call the area where Kenny was going, and why?
8. What was Kenny waiting for?
9. Where were Kenny and Byron sleeping at night?
10. Summarize what happened when Byron took Kenny into the bathroom.
11. What did Byron say Kenny should think about?
12. How did Kenny feel at the end of the story?

ANSWER KEY: Short Answer Study Guide Questions
The Watsons Go to Birmingham–1963

Chapters 1-2

1. What did Momma call Michigan?
    She called Michigan a giant icebox.

2. Where was Momma from originally?
    Momma was originally from Birmingham, Alabama.

3. What was Byron called since he turned age thirteen?
    He was called an official juvenile delinquent.

4. What did Momma do when she thought something was funny? Why did she do that?
    She put her hand over her mouth. She had a gap between her two front teeth that she did not like to show.

5. What did Dad tell the family there was in downtown Birmingham?
    He said there was a bathroom for "Coloreds Only."

6. What happened to Byron when he and Kenny were scraping the ice off the car windows?
    Byron kissed his image in the side mirror and his lips froze to the mirror.

7. What was Kenny's nickname for the family?
    He called the family The Weird Watsons.

8. What did Kenny call Byron after the incident with the ice on the car windows? Why?
    He called Byron the "Lipless Wonder" because Momma pulled his lips off the frozen mirror, removing some of the skin.

9. Whom did Kenny refer to as the king of grades K-4 and the god of the school?
    Larry Dunn was the king and his brother Byron was the god.

10. Why did the other kids tease Kenny? What did Byron tell him to do about it?
    Kenny got teased because he had a lazy eye. Byron told him to keep his head straight and look at people sideways.

11. How did Kenny think of Rufus and why?
    Kenny thought of Rufus as his personal savior because when he first met Rufus he realized that the other kids would begin teasing Rufus instead of him.

12. What did the family call the car? What kind of car was it?
    The car was a 1948 Plymouth that they called "The Brown Bomber."

Chapters 3-4

1. What did Kenny think would happen when the teacher sat Rufus next to him in class? Was he right or wrong? Explain what happened.
    He was upset. He thought that now he would get picked on even more, since they were both people who got teased anyway. He was wrong. The other kids left Kenny alone and started picking on Rufus.

2. What did Kenny find out about Rufus and his brother Cody?
    He found out that both of them had shot guns and killed squirrels.

3. Why had Kenny stopped playing with LJ Jones?
    LJ had stolen many of Kenny's toy dinosaurs.

4. Why didn't Kenny mind playing with Rufus?
    Rufus shared Kenny's interest in playing with toy dinosaurs, Rufus was willing to be the Nazi dinosaurs, and Rufus didn't cheat or steal Kenny's dinosaurs.

5. Why was Rufus upset with Kenny? What happened as a result? How did Kenny feel? How was the problem solved?
    Larry Dunn made fun of Rufus and Cody because of their pants. When the other kids laughed, Kenny laughed along with them. Rufus stopped sitting next to Kenny and playing at his house. Kenny felt sad and told his mother what had happened. His mother visited Rufus's house and the next day Rufus and Cody came over to Kenny's house. Kenny apologized and the boys became friends again.

6. Why did Momma make the children wear so many clothes in the winter?
    She was from Alabama and did not understand cold weather. She thought it would kill the children in a flash.

7. What was Byron's explanation for why they had to wear so many clothes? How did this explanation affect Joey?
    He said that if they froze to death they would be picked up by the garbage truck that collected dead, frozen people. After he told her that, Joey never whined again about wearing so many clothes.

8. Describe the game called "The Great Carp Escape." Explain who was playing it and why. Tell how Kenny felt about the game.
    Larry had stolen Kenny's good leather gloves. When Byron found out, he and Buphead got them back. They punished Larry by playing "The Great Carp Escape." This was a game where Byron made Larry act like a carp trying to get out of a net in the Flint River. Byron threw Larry against the chain link fence over and over. Kenny wished he had not told Byron about the problem with the gloves. He could not stand watching and left the schoolyard.

Chapters 5-6

1. What did Momma catch Byron doing and what did she say she would do to him?
    Byron got caught lighting matches in the bathroom. Momma said she would burn his fingers.

2. Was Momma successful in carrying out her threat? Explain why or why not.
    No, she was not. She tried to burn Byron's fingers but Joey kept blowing out the matches.

3. What did Momma tell the boys to do when they went to Mitchell's store for some groceries? What did Byron think this meant, and how did he feel about it? Was Byron's assumption correct?
    Momma told Byron to sign for the groceries. He thought that meant they were on welfare. He was embarrassed to sign a welfare list like a peon. He made Kenny sign for the food. Byron's assumption was not correct. The family was not on welfare. Mr. Watson had arranged to pay the bill all at once.

4. What did Byron do after he found out the truth about the list at Mitchell's store?
    He started signing for food for himself, including boxes of Swedish Creme cookies.

5. Describe what happened to the mourning dove.
    Byron threw Swedish Creme cookies at it and killed it. Kenny saw it happen. Byron got sick and then angry with Kenny. He threw apples from the tree at Kenny. Kenny ran out of the alley but went back a little while later. He discovered that Byron had dug a grave and buried the dove.

Chapters 7-8

1. What did Byron do to his hair? What did Momma say about it? What was Byron's reason for doing it?
    Byron got a conk, or process, which meant that he chemically straightened his hair. Momma sent Byron to his room and said that Byron would be at his father's mercy. Byron said he did it because he wanted a Mexican hairstyle.

2. What did Dad do about Byron's hair? What song did he whistle during the process?
    Dad shaved Byron's head bald while whistling, "Straighten Up and Fly Right."

3. What did Dad tell Byron after the punishment had been completed?
    Dad told Byron that he had been told enough, and this time something would be done.

4. Who is Grandma Sands?
    She is Mrs. Watson's mother.

5. Kenny described his parents as acting strange after they talked to Grandma Sands. What were they doing?
   Momma was writing in a notebook and adding and subtracting things. Dad was taking Kenny, Joey, and Rufus with him all over Flint buying things for the car.

6. Dad bought something very special for the car that he asked Joey to put on the car. What was it and how did Dad describe it?
   It was a smelly green pine tree. Dad described it as "the pinnacle of Western Civilization" and "the ultimate in American knowledge."

7. There was something in the Watson house that Dad did not keep with the ones that belonged to the rest of the family. What was it, and why did Dad keep his separate?
   Dad did not keep his toothbrush with those of the rest of the family. He said that he knew that little boys liked to use toothbrushes for cleaning and other things.

8. What did Dad put in the car? How did Momma react when she saw it? What did the children think?
   Dad installed a drive-around record player called the True-Tone AB-700 Ultra Glide. At first Momma was upset and went back in the house. Then she came back out and they all listened to records. The children liked it.

9. What was Momma's song? What was Kenny's song?
   Momma's song was "Under the Boardwalk." Kenny's song was "Yakety Yak."

10. What news did the parents tell the children while they were all sitting in the car listening to the records? What were their reasons for this news?
    The parents told the children that the family would soon be driving to Alabama. Byron would be spending the summer or maybe the next school year with Grandma Sands. They said that Byron was driving them crazy and they would not have the nonsense going on any more.

Chapters 9-10
1. Dad talked with Kenny about the reasons they were sending Byron to Alabama. What did Dad tell Kenny?
   Dad told Kenny that Byron was learning things they didn't want him to learn, and he was not learning the things they wanted him to learn. They thought that spending some time in the South would open Byron's eyes to the way the world could be; that there were not a lot of jokes waiting for Byron when he got older.

2. How did Kenny feel when Dad talked to him like a grown-up?
   He loved it, even though he did not always understand what Dad said.

3. Summarize the incident when Mrs. Davidson gave a gift to Joey.
   Mrs. Davidson gave Joey a little angel figurine that she said reminded her of Joey. Joey politely thanked her, but later told her mother that she didn't like the angel because it was white, and she was not a white girl.

4. Where did Byron have to sleep the night before the family left on the trip, and why?
   He had to sleep on the floor in his parents' room. Joey had told them that Byron was planning to run away that night, so they were preventing that from happening.

5. On the trip, Kenny asked why they could not drive until Dad was tired and then stop for the day. What was Dad's reply? How did he sound when he answered?
   Dad answered in a hillbilly accent. He said that since they were in the South there were places that colored folks would not be able to stop.

6. What was the title of Momma's notebook? What was on the cover? What were the contents?
   Momma called her notebook, "The Watsons Go to Birmingham–1963. She drew a bee and a flower on the cover. Inside, she had written down plans for the trip; where, when, and what they would eat, how much money they would spend, when they would take rest and bathroom stops, who got the windows each day, and who would clean up the car.

7. How did Byron plan to pay his parents back for making him go to Alabama? Was he successful?
   He planned to not talk to anyone for the entire trip. He did not follow through with his plan. By the time they got to Detroit, Byron asked how they were going to work the record player.

8. Dad planned ahead of time to do something on the trip but not tell Momma. What was it?
   Dad had planned to drive the fifteen hours straight through instead of taking three days.

9. Kenny described something on their trip as the scariest things he had ever seen. What were they? Why did he think these things were scary?
   They were the Appalachian Mountains. He said they were the biggest, blackest hills ever, and it looked like the family was in a pitch-black blanket.

10. How did Dad describe driving through the mountains?
    He said they had their fingers in God's beard and were tickling him as they drove.

Chapters 11-12

1. What made Kenny think that Dad was very tired?
    Dad was talking a lot and that was unusual for him.

2. Kenny thought that Birmingham looked a lot like another place. What place was that? What surprised Kenny about Birmingham?
    He thought it looked a lot like Flint. He was surprised to see real houses, not log cabins, and he liked the trees and the sun.

3. What did Kenny expect Grandma Sands to look like? What did she really look like?
    He expected a troll. He thought she would be bigger than Dad and foaming at the mouth. Instead, she was a very small old woman who looked like a shrunken version of his mother.

4. What fictional characters did Kenny use to describe how he expected the meeting between Grandma Sands and Byron to go? What characters did he use to describe how the meeting actually went? How did Kenny feel about the reality of the meeting?
    Kenny thought the meeting would be like King Kong meeting Godzilla. Instead it was like King Kong meets Bambi. Kenny thought it was like all the fight was out of Byron.

5. How did Kenny describe Birmingham?
    He said it was like an oven.

6. Who was Mr. Robert?
    Mr. Robert was Grandma Sands's companion and dearest friend. He helped her around the house.

7. What took the children a while to get used to?
    It took them a while to get used to the Southern way of talking.

8. What did Kenny think about making Byron spend a whole summer in the heat? How did Byron seem to be taking it?
    Kenny thought that spending the whole summer in the heat was more than even Byron deserved. Byron seemed like he was enjoying himself.

Chapters 13-14

1. What place were the children told to stay away from and why?
    They were told to stay away from Collier's Landing because a little boy had got caught up in a whirlpool and drowned there.

2. How did Byron describe the whirlpool?
    He called it a "Wool Pooh" and said it was Winnie the Pooh's evil twin brother. It would hide under the water and snatch kids down under the water.

3. Where did Kenny go? Did Byron and Joey go with him?
    Kenny went to Collier's Landing anyway. Byron and Joey did not go with him.

4. Describe what happened to Kenny when he went in the water.
    He waded out to catch a fish and he got caught in the whirlpool. Byron and Joey saved him.

5. What did Byron do when Kenny was out of the water?
    Byron kept repeating, "Kenny, Kenny" and kissing the top of Kenny's head.

6. What was the noise that Kenny and the others heard?
    It was a bomb that someone threw at the church where Joey had gone that morning.

7. Describe what Kenny did and saw when he got to the church.
    He went inside and saw smoke and dust. He saw a shiny black shoe under some concrete and pulled on it. Then he thought he saw the Wool Pooh again. He grabbed the shoe and left the church with it. Then he went back to Grandma Sands's house.

8. Describe the conversation between Joey and Kenny back at Grandma Sands's house.
    Joey asked Kenny how he got back home so fast and why he changed his clothes. Kenny thought that the Wool Pooh was taking Joey around to say good-bye. Kenny thanked Joey for saving his life. Joey asked him if he was crazy. Then Joey asked him whose shoe he had with him, since she was carrying both of hers.

9. What did Joey tell Kenny about her time in the church that morning?
    She said it was hot so she went outside. She saw Kenny and chased him down the street.

10. What did Kenny realize when Grandma Sands asked where his parents were? What did he do then?
    He realized that the Wool Pooh had missed Joey after all. He went back to the church to get his parents and Byron.

Chapter 15
1. Who threw the bomb?
    Two white men in a car threw the bomb.

2. Who was killed and injured?
    Four little girls were killed, a few people were blinded, and others were sent to the hospital with other injuries.

3. How did Kenny's parents take the bombing?
    They were mad, then sometimes calm, and other times they sat and cried.

4. When and why did the family leave Birmingham?
    They left the night of the bombing before Joey could find out what had happened.

5. Which one of the children were the parents the most worried about? Why?
    They were most worried about Kenny. They wondered if Mr. Robert's friend had been right when he told them he had seen Kenny in the church after the bombing.

6. Where was Kenny going when he disappeared?
    He was hiding behind the couch in the living room every day.

7. What did Byron call the area where Kenny was going, and why?
    Byron called the area behind the couch the World Famous Watson Pet Hospital because that was where their various pets had gone when they were sick.

8. What was Kenny waiting for?
    He was waiting for some magic powers to come and make him feel better.

9. Where were Kenny and Byron sleeping at night?
    Kenny was sleeping behind the couch and Byron was sleeping on the couch.

10. Summarize what happened when Bryon took Kenny into the bathroom.
    Byron took Kenny into the bathroom to show him a hair on his (Byron's) chin. When Kenny looked in the mirror and saw himself looking so sad he started crying. He asked Byron why the men would want to hurt kids by bombing the church. Kenny said he was ashamed because he left Joey in the church when he thought the Wool Pooh had her.

11. What did Byron say Kenny should think about?
    He said Kenny should think about why Joey was not in the church. He said it was a part of Kenny that took Joey out of the church.

12. How did Kenny feel at the end of the story?
    He felt better and was laughing.

MULTIPLE CHOICE STUDY GUIDE QUESTIONS
The Watsons Go to Birmingham–1963

Chapters 1-2
1. What did Momma call Michigan?
    A. She called Michigan a northern paradise.
    B. She called Michigan the end of nowhere.
    C. She called Michigan a giant icebox.
    D. She called Michigan a crowded, unfriendly place.

2. Where was Momma from originally?
    A. She was from Birmingham, Alabama.
    B. She was from Los Angeles, California.
    C. She was from Nashville, Tennessee.
    D. She was from New York City, New York.

3. What was Byron called since he turned age thirteen?
    A. He was called "Young Master Watson."
    B. He was called "By the Guy."
    C. He was called the heir to the Watson fortune.
    D. He was called an official juvenile delinquent.

4. Why did Momma put her hand over her mouth when she thought something was funny?
    A. She had been raised that it was not proper for a lady to laugh.
    B. She had a gap between her two front teeth that she did not like to show.
    C. She did not like the sound of her giggle and tried to stop it.
    D. She did not like to show her emotions.

5. What did Dad tell the family there was in downtown Birmingham?
    A. He said there was a statue of Harriet Tubman.
    B. He said there was an old slave auction block with chains on it.
    C. He said there was a bathroom for "Coloreds Only."
    D. He said there was a garden dedicated to Abraham Lincoln.

6. What happened to Byron when he and Kenny were scraping the ice off the car windows?
    A. Byron kissed his image in the side mirror and his lips froze to the mirror.
    B. Kenny rubbed the side window glass so hard that he put his hand through it.
    C. Byron pushed the back of the car and it rolled down the street.
    D. Kenny worked faster than Byron and Byron got angry.

Multiple Choice Study Guide Questions *The Watsons Go to Birmingham–1963*
Chapters 1-2, continued

7. What was Kenny's nickname for the family?
    A. He called the family "The Watson Wackos."
    B. He called the family "The Wunnaful, Wunnaful Watsons."
    C. He called the family "Watch Out for the Watsons."
    D. He called the family "The Weird Watsons."

8. What did Kenny call Byron after the incident with the ice on the car windows?
    A. He called Byron the "Iceman."
    B. He called Byron the "Lipless Wonder."
    C. He called Byron the "Slowpoke."
    D. He called Byron the "Supreme Roller."

9. Whom did Kenny refer to as the king of grades K-4 and the god of the school?
    A. Larry Dunn was the king and Byron was the god.
    B. Byron was the king and Buphead was the god.
    C. Kenny was the king and Larry Dunn was the god.
    D. Buphead was the king and Byron was the god.

10. Why did the other kids tease Kenny?
    A. Kenny got teased because the other kids were afraid to tease Byron.
    B. Kenny got teased because he had a big nose.
    C. Kenny got teased because he had a lazy eye.
    D. Kenny got teased because he was so much smarter than all of the others.

11. How did Kenny think of Rufus?
    A. Kenny thought of Rufus as a country hick.
    B. Kenny thought of Rufus as his personal savior.
    C. Kenny thought of Rufus as a kind and gentle person.
    D. Kenny thought of Rufus as a wild rebel.

12. What did the family call the car? What kind of car was it?
    A. The car was a 1935 Ford that they called "The Golden Wings."
    B. The car was a 1956 Chrysler that they called "The Green Beetle."
    C. The car was a 1962 Chevrolet that they called "The Scarlet Rocket."
    D. The car was a 1948 Plymouth that they called "The Brown Bomber."

Multiple Choice Study Guide Questions *The Watsons Go to Birmingham–1963*

<u>Chapters 3-4</u>

1. True or False: After Rufus began sitting next to Kenny in class, both boys got picked on.
    A. True
    B. False

2. What did Kenny find out about Rufus and his brother Cody?
    A. He found out that both of them had lice.
    B. He found out that both of them had been left back twice.
    C. He found out that both of them had been adopted.
    D. He found out that both of them had shot guns and killed squirrels.

3. True or False: Kenny stopped playing with LJ Jones because LJ had stolen many of Kenny's toy dinosaurs.
    A. True
    B. False

4. Kenny didn't mind playing with one other child because this person shared Kenny's interest in playing with toy dinosaurs, was willing to be the Nazi dinosaurs, and didn't cheat or steal Kenny's dinosaurs. Who was this child?
    A. Joey
    B. Rufus
    C. Wilona
    D. Ward

5. Why was Rufus upset with Kenny?
    A. Kenny would not share his lunch dessert with Cody and Rufus.
    B. Kenny invited Rufus to play but would not invite Cody. Since Rufus had to watch over Cody, then Rufus could not go to Kenny's house.
    C. Larry Dunn made fun of Rufus and Cody because of their pants. When the other kids laughed, Kenny laughed along with them.
    D. The teacher told Rufus to help Kenny with some math. Kenny got insulted and refused to let Rufus help.

6. What did Momma make the children do in the winter?
    A. Momma made the children stay in the house all of the time.
    B. Momma made the children sleep in the same bed with their parents.
    C. Momma made the children say extra prayers to keep them from freezing.
    D. Momma made the children wear many layers of clothes when they went out.

Multiple Choice Study Guide Questions *The Watsons Go to Birmingham–1963*

Chapters 3-4, continued

7. What did Byron tell Joey about people who froze to death in the winter?
    A. He said that if they froze to death they would be picked up by the garbage truck that collected dead, frozen people.
    B. He said they went to a special place where they thawed out before they were sent to heaven or hell.
    C. He said the city gave the frozen person's family all new winter clothes to make sure that no one else in the family froze.
    D. He said they froze because they were not smart enough to stay inside.

8. What happened to Kenny's good leather gloves?
    A. LJ took them and sold them to get money for toys.
    B. Larry had stolen them and was wearing them.
    C. Joey used them to swat at a stray dog and the dog got them.
    D. Kenny traded them to Buphead for protection against another mean boy.

9. Who played "The Great Carp Escape," and how did they play?
    A. Larry threw things that belonged to the other boys in the lake and other boys ran in to get them. When they tried to get out of the lake, Larry hit them with rocks.
    B. LJ stole things from the other boys. To get them back, the boys had to pay and also do several jobs for LJ.
    C. Byron and Buphead threw someone who had bothered Kenny against the chain link fence over and over. The boy was supposed to try and get away.
    D. Boys from the high school put boys from the elementary school in fishing nets and hung them in trees. The boys had to get themselves out of the nets.

10. True or False: Kenny could not stand watching and left the area.
    A. True
    B. False

Multiple Choice Study Guide Questions *The Watsons Go to Birmingham–1963*

Chapters 5-6
1. What did Momma catch Byron doing?
    A. Byron got caught smoking cigarettes in back of the house.
    B. Byron got caught lighting matches in the bathroom.
    C. Byron got caught stealing money from his mother's purse.
    D. Byron got caught forging Dad's signature on his report card.

2. What did Momma say she would do to Byron because of his actions?
    A. Momma said she would make him visit the cancer ward at the hospital.
    B. Momma said she would report Byron to the police.
    C. Momma said she would burn his fingers.
    D. Momma said Byron would have to spend a month in his room.

3. Was Momma successful in carrying out her threat?
    A. No, she was not.
    B. Yes, she was.

4. What did Momma tell Byron to do when he went to Mr. Mitchell's store?
    A. She told him to use money from his piggy bank to pay.
    B. She told him to offer to work for Mr. Mitchell in payment for the food.
    C. She told him to ask if he could pay the next week.
    D. She told him to sign for the groceries.

5. True or False: The family was on welfare.
    A. True
    B. False

6. What did Byron do after he found out the truth about the list at Mitchell's store?
    A. He refused to go shopping for the family.
    B. He stopped eating desserts to save money.
    C. He started buying food for himself.
    D. He started shopping at a different store.

7. How did the mourning dove die?
    A. Kenny chased it and it crashed into a store window.
    B. Byron threw Swedish Creme cookies at it and killed it.
    C. It ate popcorn that the boys left for it and got sick.
    D. Cody killed it with his slingshot.

8. What happened to the mourning dove's body?
    A. Byron dug a grave and buried it.
    B. Kenny and Rufus burned the body and sprinkled the ashes on the playground.
    C. Cody and Rufus took it home.
    D. Kenny put it in his family's freezer.

Multiple Choice Study Guide Questions *The Watsons Go to Birmingham–1963*

Chapters 7-8

1. What did Byron do to his hair?
    A. He dyed his hair blue to match the school colors.
    B. He got his name shaved into the back of his head.
    C. He braided it and put beads in it.
    D. He got a conk, or chemically straightened his hair.

2. What did his parents do about Bryon's new hairdo?
    A. Dad shaved Byron's head bald.
    B. Momma took him to her hairdresser to get it fixed.
    C. They said he would have to live with it.
    D. They made Byron wear a dress until the hair was back to normal.

3. What did Dad tell Byron after the punishment had been completed?
    A. Dad told Byron that his behavior hurt him more than it hurt the family.
    B. Dad told Byron that they were going to send him to a strict military school.
    C. Dad told Byron that he had been told enough, and something would be done.
    D. Dad told Byron that his behavior was immature and he should grow up.

4. Who is Grandma Sands?
    A. She is Mr. Watson's grandmother.
    B. She is Mrs. Watson's mother.
    C. She is Mrs. Watson's grandmother.
    D. She is Mr. Watson's aunt.

5. Kenny described his parents as acting strange after they talked to Grandma Sands. What were they doing?
    A. Momma was writing in a notebook and adding and subtracting things. Dad was going all over Flint buying things for the car.
    B. Momma went out and got a job. Dad started working two jobs.
    C. Momma cleaned the house from top to bottom. Dad repaired broken things and painted the inside of the house.
    D. Dad began working overtime and Momma cut down on the amount of food she served at each meal.

6. Dad described something as "the pinnacle of Western Civilization" and "the ultimate in American knowledge." What was it?
    A. It was the latest edition of the *Encyclopedia Britannica*.
    B. It was a college education.
    C. It was a smelly green pine tree for the car.
    D. It was a television set.

Multiple Choice Study Guide Questions *The Watsons Go to Birmingham–1963*

Chapters 7-8

7. There was something in the Watson house that Dad did not keep with the ones that belonged to the rest of the family. What was it?
    A. It was Dad's shoes.
    B. It was Dad's toothbrush.
    C. It was Dad's coffee mug.
    D. It was Dad's laundry.

8. What did Dad put in the car?
    A. It was a side-view mirror on the passenger's side.
    B. It was new cup holders in the front and the back.
    C. It was a personal license plate that said, "BRNBMR."
    D. It was a drive-around record player.

9. What was Momma's song? What was Kenny's song?
    A. Momma's song was "Love Me Tender." Kenny's song was "Big Bad John."
    B. Momma's song was "Ebony Eyes." Kenny's song was "Blue Suede Shoes."
    C. Momma's song was "Under the Boardwalk." Kenny's song was "Yakety Yak."
    D. Momma's song was "Up on the Roof." Kenny's song was "Beep Beep."

10. While they were all sitting in the car, the parents told the children the family____.
    A. would soon be driving to Alabama. Byron would be spending the summer or maybe the next school with Grandma Sands.
    B. would soon be driving to New York. Byron would be attending military school there. Grandma Sands was paying for it.
    C. would soon be moving to Alabama. The family was going to move in with Grandma Sands.
    D. would soon be moving to Montana. They bought a ranch so the children would not be exposed to city life any more. Grandma Sands would move in with them.

Multiple Choice Study Guide Questions *The Watsons Go to Birmingham–1963*

Chapters 9-10

1. Dad talked with Kenny about the reasons they were sending Byron to Alabama. What did Dad tell Kenny?
    - A. Grandma Sands had raised ten boys and they were all fine men. The parents thought she could get Byron to straighten up.
    - B. Byron was taking up too much of their time and attention. They were sending him away so they could concentrate on raising the other two children.
    - C. They thought that spending some time in the South would open Byron's eyes to the way the world could be.
    - D. They felt like failures as parents and needed help.

2. How did Kenny feel when Dad talked to him like a grown-up?
    - A. He loved it.
    - B. It scared him.

3. Which statement about the gift from Mrs. Davidson to Joey is true?
    - A. Joey didn't like the large stuffed dog because it scared her.
    - B. Joey didn't like the angel because it was white, and she was not a white girl.
    - C. Joey liked the new dress and put it on right away.
    - D. Joey liked the mystery book and began reading it.

4. Where did Byron have to sleep the night before the family left on the trip?
    - A. He had to sleep in his parent's closet.
    - B. He had to sleep at the police station.
    - C. He had to sleep at Buphead's house.
    - D. He had to sleep on the floor in his parents' room.

5. On the trip, Kenny asked why they could not drive until Dad was tired and then stop for the day. Dad said ____.
    - A. they did not have enough money for a motel room.
    - B. it was not good for the car's engine to stop because the car was so old.
    - C. there were places in the South that colored folks would not be able to stop.
    - D. they were in a big hurry to see Grandma Sands because she was sick.

6. Which statement does not describe something about Momma's notebook?
    - A. The title of the notebook was "The Weird Watsons on the Road."
    - B. She had drawn a bee and a flower on the cover.
    - C. Inside, she had written down plans for the trip, including expenses.
    - D. She had a list of who got the windows each day.

Multiple Choice Study Guide Questions *The Watsons Go to Birmingham–1963*

Chapters 9-10, continued

7. Byron planned to not talk to anyone for the entire trip, to pay his parents back for taking him to Alabama. Was he successful?
    A. Yes
    B. No

8. Dad planned ahead of time to do something on the trip but not tell Momma. What was it?
    A. Dad had planned to sell the car and buy a new one.
    B. Dad had planned to stop for two days in the mountains.
    C. Dad had planned to drive straight through.
    D. Dad had planned to pick up a cousin in Tennessee.

9. Kenny described the ____ as the scariest things he had ever seen.
    A. mountain folks in a pick-up truck
    B. Appalachian Mountains
    C. black bears at a rest stop
    D. signs that said, "Whites Only"

10. Dad described the ____ by saying the family had their fingers in God's beard and were tickling him as they drove.
    A. fog
    B. snow
    C. farmland
    D. mountains

Multiple Choice Study Guide Questions *The Watsons Go to Birmingham–1963*

<u>Chapters 11-12</u>

1. What made Kenny think that Dad was very tired?
    A. Dad was closing his eyes and telling Bryon to steer.
    B. Dad was shaking his head a lot.
    C. Dad was talking a lot.
    D. Dad was yawning and stretching.

2. True or False: Kenny thought that Birmingham looked a lot like Flint.
    A. True
    B. False

3. Did Grandma Sands look the way Kenny expected her to look?
    A. Yes, she did.
    B. No, she did not.

4. What fictional characters did Kenny use to describe how he expected the meeting between Grandma Sands and Byron to go? What characters did he use to describe how the meeting actually went?
    A. Kenny thought the meeting would be like Popeye meeting Brutus. Instead it was like Popeye meets Olive Oyl.
    B. Kenny thought the meeting would be like Tarzan meeting the lion. Instead it was like Tarzan meets Jane.
    C. Kenny thought the meeting would be like Superman meeting Lex Luthor. Instead it was like Superman meets Ma Kent.
    D. Kenny thought the meeting would be like King Kong meeting Godzilla. Instead it was like King Kong meets Bambi.

5. What did Kenny think about the meeting between Grandma Sands and Byron?
    A. He thought all the fight was out of Byron.
    B. He thought Byron was acting tough.
    C. He thought that Byron was being polite until he figured out what to do.
    D. He thought that Byron was terrified of Grandma Sands.

6. How did Kenny describe Birmingham?
    A. He said it was like an oven.
    B. He said it was the dullest place he had ever seen.
    C. He said it was like Flint in prehistoric times.
    D. He said it was like a swamp.

Multiple Choice Study Guide Questions *The Watsons Go to Birmingham–1963*

Chapters 11-12, continued

7. Who was Grandma Sands's companion and dearest friend?
    A. Mr. Bruce
    B. Mr. Moses
    C. Mr. Robert
    D. Mr. Albert

8. It took them a while to get used to the Southern ____.
    A. way of talking
    B. food
    C. mosquitoes
    D. politeness

9. What did Kenny think about making Byron spend a whole summer in the heat?
    A. Kenny thought that the punishment was just right for Byron.
    B. Kenny thought that Byron deserved a whole year of the heat.
    C. Kenny thought that Byron had already been punished enough.
    D. Kenny thought it was more than even Byron deserved.

10. True or False: Byron acted like he could not stand being in Alabama.
    A. True
    B. False

Multiple Choice Study Guide Questions *The Watsons Go to Birmingham–1963*

Chapters 13-14

1. The children told to stay away from ___ because a boy had drowned in the whirlpool.
    A. Burton's Bayou
    B. Collier's Landing
    C. Marion's Swamp
    D. Dragon's Marsh

2. Which statement describes the way Byron described the whirlpool?
    A. It was called a Whirled Poor and grabbed poor children.
    B. It was called a Devil's Net and caught children who had disobeyed.
    C. It was called a Wool Pooh and was Winnie the Pooh's evil twin brother.
    D. It was called the Worse Pull and was a cousin of the Swamp Thing.

3. True or False: Kenny went to the forbidden place but Byron and Joey did not.
    A. True
    B. False

4. _____ saved Kenny.
    A. Mr. Robert
    B. Dad
    C. the paramedics
    D. Byron and Joey

5. What did Byron do when Kenny was out of the water?
    A. Bryon beat up Kenny for being reckless.
    B. Bryon ran home to get towels and a blanket.
    C. Byron kissed the top of Kenny's head.
    D. Bryon gave Kenny CPR to help him breathe again.

6. What was the noise that Kenny and the others heard?
    A. It was a sonic boom from an airplane.
    B. It was a tornado.
    C. It was a cannon.
    D. It was a bomb.

7. Which statement about what Kenny did and saw when he got to the church is <u>false</u>?
    A. He went inside and saw smoke and dust.
    B. He pulled a dead girl out by her legs.
    C. He grabbed the shoe and left the church with it.
    D. He thought he saw the water monster with Joey.

Multiple Choice Study Guide Questions *The Watsons Go to Birmingham–1963*

Chapters 13-14, continued

8. Who asked Kenny how he got back home so fast and why he changed his clothes?
    A. Joey
    B. Grandma Sands
    C. Byron
    D. Momma

9. What did Joey tell Kenny about her time in the church that morning?
    A. She said she ran when she heard the noise.
    B. She said she had gone to the park instead of church.
    C. She said saw Kenny and chased him down the street.
    D. She said she came home early because she was tired.

10. True or False: Kenny hid under the bed and would not go back to the church.
    A. True
    B. False

Multiple Choice Study Guide Questions *The Watsons Go to Birmingham–1963*

Chapter 15

1. ____ threw the bomb.
    A. Two white men
    B. Three black teenagers
    C. Four Hispanic men
    D. One Muslim suicide bomber

2. ____ were killed.
    A. Seven teenage boys
    B. Four little girls
    C. Twelve older men and women
    D. Fifty women

3. Who got mad, then sometimes calm, and other times sat and cried after the bombing?
    A. Mr. Robert
    B. Grandma Sands
    C. Momma and Dad
    D. Byron and Joey

4. When did the family leave Birmingham?
    A. They left a month after the bombing.
    B. They left the next morning.
    C. They left the night of the bombing.
    D. They left in a week, right after the funerals.

5. Who were the parents the most worried about?
    A. Joey
    B. Grandma Sands
    C. Byron
    D. Kenny

6. Where was Kenny going when he disappeared every day?
    A. He was hiding behind the couch in the living room.
    B. He was going up into the attic.
    C. He was going out into the garage under the woodpile.
    D. He was going under the back porch.

7. Byron called the area where Kenny was going the ____.
    A. Watson Feel Better Quick Club
    B. World Famous Watson Pet Hospital
    C. Watson Forget Your Troubles Room
    D. Kenny Watson Care Center

Multiple Choice Study Guide Questions *The Watsons Go to Birmingham–1963*

Chapter 15, continued

8. What was Kenny waiting for?
    A. He was waiting for the dark cloud over his head to break up.
    B. He was waiting for his mother to tell him that things were fine.
    C. He was waiting for some magic powers to come and make him feel better.
    D. He was waiting for the minister to come and tell him the girls were in heaven.

9. Where were Kenny and Byron sleeping at night?
    A. They were both sleeping in Byron's bed.
    B. Kenny was sleeping behind the couch and Byron was sleeping on the couch.
    C. They were sleeping in a tent in the back yard.
    D. Kenny was sleeping with his parents and Byron was sleeping in Joey's room.

10. What did Kenny tell Byron when they were in the bathroom?
    A. Kenny said he was ashamed because he left Joey in the church.
    B. Kenny said he had nightmares about the blood and the smoke.
    C. Kenny said he thought he would never get better.
    D. Kenny said that if Byron had not misbehaved they would not have been in Birmingham.

11. True or False: Byron said it was a part of Kenny that took Joey out of the church.
    A. True
    B. False

12. How did Kenny feel at the end of the story?
    A. He was sadder than ever and cried all the time.
    B. He felt better and was laughing.
    C. He was angry.
    D. He was scared and lonely.

ANSWER KEY MULTIPLE CHOICE STUDY GUIDE/QUIZ QUESTIONS
The Watsons Go to Birmingham–1963

	Chapters 1-2	Chapters 3-4	Chapters 5-6	Chapters 7-8
1	C	B	B	D
2	A	D	C	A
3	D	A	A	C
4	B	B	D	B
5	C	C	B	A
6	A	D	C	C
7	D	A	B	B
8	B	B	A	D
9	A	C		C
10	C	A		A
11	B			
12	D			

	Chapters 9-10	Chapters 11-12	Chapters 13-14	Chapter 15
1	C	C	B	A
2	A	A	C	B
3	B	B	A	C
4	D	D	D	C
5	C	A	C	D
6	A	A	D	A
7	B	C	B	B
8	C	A	A	C
9	B	D	C	B
10	D	B	B	A
11				A
12				B

PREREADING VOCABULARY WORKSHEETS

Prereading Vocabulary Worksheets *The Watsons Go to Birmingham–1963*

Chapters 1-2

Part I: Using Prior Knowledge and Contextual Clues
Below are the sentences in which the vocabulary words appear in the text. Read the sentence. Use any clues you can find in the sentence combined with your prior knowledge, and write what you think the underlined word means in the space provided.

1. Dad said this would generate a little heat but he didn't have to tell us this . . .

2. "Ain't got nothing against 'em, but don't believe you'd be too happy living 'mongst a whole slew of Chinese folks."

3. Dad thought that was hilarious and put his head back on his arm.

4. "I've often told you that as Negroes the world is many times a hostile place for us."

5. "I've pointed out time and time again how vital it is that one be able to read well."

6. "And Byron Watson, if you are incapable of taking some of the fire out of your eyes I assure you I will find a way to assist you."

7. "If, instead of trying to intimidate your young brother, you would emulate him and use that mind of yours, perhaps you would find things much easier."

8. If, instead of trying to intimidate your young brother, you would emulate him and use that mind of yours, perhaps you would find things much easier."

9. We'd be standing on the corner waiting for the bus, Byron, Buphead and all the other old thugs in one bunch.

10. "This is the only way you little punks is gonna learn to be punctual. I hope that fool has a pleasant walk to school."

Prereading Vocabulary Worksheets *The Watsons Go to Birmingham–1963*

<u>Chapters 1-2</u>

Part II: Determining the Meaning:
  Match the vocabulary words to their dictionary definitions.

_____ 1. generate   A. very funny

_____ 2. slew   B. not able to do something

_____ 3. hilarious   C. gangsters; violent criminals

_____ 4. hostile   D. produce or make

_____ 5. vital   E. try to be like someone else

_____ 6. incapable   F. full of hatred or anger

_____ 7. intimidate   G. on time

_____ 8. emulate   H. create a feeling of fear in someone

_____ 9. thugs   I. a large number

_____ 10. punctual   J. very important

Prereading Vocabulary Worksheets *The Watsons Go to Birmingham–1963*

Chapters 3-4

Part I: Using Prior Knowledge and Contextual Clues
Below are the sentences in which the vocabulary words appear in the text. Read the sentence. Use any clues you can find in the sentence combined with your prior knowledge, and write what you think the underlined word means in the space provided.

1. This guy was real desperate for a friend because even though I wouldn't say much back to him he kept jabbering away at me all through class.
   _____

2. "It was the radioactiveness. We gotta bury the dead before they infect the rest of the live ones."
   _____

3. She got so hot inside all this stuff that when I finally got down to the last layer she'd be soaking wet and kind of drowsy-looking.
   _____

4. Joey looked like she was hypnotized. Her mouth was open and her eyes were bugging.
   _____

5. I just about broke out laughing when she held me by the arms and looked right in my eyes and said, "Do you know what frostbite will do to you?"
   _____

6. . . . I acted like I had been popped by Sugar Ray Robinson and I staggered around, then fell on my knees holding my stomach.
   _____

7. *The Great Carp Escape* was about a carp that was trying to get out of a net in the Flint River.
   _____

Prereading Vocabulary Worksheets *The Watsons Go to Birmingham–1963*

Chapters 3-4

Part II: Determining the Meaning:
Match the vocabulary words to their dictionary definitions.

_____ 1. jabbering   A. walked unsteadily

_____ 2. infect   B. talking very quickly

_____ 3. drowsy   C. damage to limbs caused by freezing

_____ 4. hypnotized   D. sleepy

_____ 5. staggered   E. a breed of large fish, including goldfish

_____ 6. frostbite   F. put into a sleep-like condition

_____ 7. carp   G. give a disease to

Prereading Vocabulary Worksheets *The Watsons Go to Birmingham–1963*

Chapters 5-6

Part I: Using Prior Knowledge and Contextual Clues
Below are the sentences in which the vocabulary words appear in the text. Read the sentence. Use any clues you can find in the sentence combined with your prior knowledge, and write what you think the underlined word means in the space provided.

1. Even though the story made Momma and Joey get all sad and sobby it was kind of funny to me and By.
   _____

2. Joey climbed off Momma's lap and Byron's eyes got bigger but his traitor hands kept him pinned to the couch.
   _____

3. "Wait a minute! I know what this mean-we on welfare, ain't we?"
   _____

4. "You really gonna make me go embarrass myself by signing a welfare list for some groceries like a blanged peon?"
   _____

5. Leave it to Daddy Cool to torture human kids at school all day long and never have his conscience bother him but to feel sorry for a stupid little grayish brown bird.
   _____

6. Leave it to Daddy Cool to torture human kids at school all day long and never have his conscience bother him but to feel sorry for a stupid little grayish brown bird.
   _____

Prereading Vocabulary Worksheets *The Watsons Go to Birmingham–1963*

Chapters 5-6

Part II: Determining the Meaning:
Match the vocabulary words to their dictionary definitions.

_____ 1. sobby   A. sense of right and wrong

_____ 2. traitor   B. very low-paid worker

_____ 3. welfare   C. full of tears; crying

_____ 4. peon   D. to give pain or make to suffer

_____ 5. torture   E. aid in the form of money and other benefits

_____ 6. conscience   F. one who does something disloyal

Prereading Vocabulary Worksheets *The Watsons Go to Birmingham–1963*

Chapters 7-8

Part I: Using Prior Knowledge and Contextual Clues
Below are the sentences in which the vocabulary words appear in the text. Read the sentence. Use any clues you can find in the sentence combined with your prior knowledge, and write what you think the underlined word means in the space provided.

1. Byron had gotten a conk! A process! A do! A butter! A ton of trouble!
_____

2. "Well, let's just say I'm numb."
_____

3. Wow! He must have really felt like he didn't have anything to lose, 'cause Momma and Dad just didn't tolerate mumbling.
_____

4. Wow! He must have really felt like he didn't have anything to lose, 'cause Momma and Dad just didn't tolerate mumbling.
_____

5. Byron stepped into the living room with a real mean scowl on his face.
_____

6. Joey laughed because she was relieved Byron hadn't been executed, Momma and Dad laughed at Byron's ears, but none of them laughed as hard as me.
_____

7. Dad started shaving. "Well, just so there's no problems, I've got seniority on you, so I get the bathroom first, deal?"
_____

8. "Well, well, well," Dad said, leaning down into the car, "I see you three have the ultimate in taste."
_____

9. "Before I dazzle you with the symphonic sound of this unit, let me point out some of its less-appreciated features."
_____

Prereading Vocabulary Worksheets *The Watsons Go to Birmingham–1963*

Chapters 7-8

10. "And I can tell by that intelligent look on your face, Mrs. Watson, that you have grasped that the speaker is not placed in the rear deck <u>haphazardly</u>, no, ma'am."

_____

Part II: Determining the Meaning: Match the vocabulary words to their dictionary definitions.

_____ 1. conk   A. angry expression

_____ 2. numb   B. put to death

_____ 3. tolerate   C. unplanned

_____ 4. mumbling   D. a style that straightens curly hair

_____ 5. scowl   E. having greater age or higher rank

_____ 6. executed   F. not able to feel emotions

_____ 7. seniority   G. amaze

_____ 8. ultimate   H. put up with

_____ 9. dazzle   I. highest quality

_____ 10. haphazardly   J. speaking unclearly

Prereading Vocabulary Worksheets *The Watsons Go to Birmingham–1963*

Chapters 9-10

Part I: Using Prior Knowledge and Contextual Clues
Below are the sentences in which the vocabulary words appear in the text. Read the sentence. Use any clues you can find in the sentence combined with your prior knowledge, and write what you think the underlined word means in the space provided.

1. We listened to a couple of jive songs and then I said, "Dad, does Byron really have to go to Alabama?"
   _____

2. "Momma and I are very worried because there're so many things that can go wrong to a young person and Byron seems bound and determined to find every one of them."
   _____

3. "Momma and I are very worried because there're so many things that can go wrong to a young person and Byron seems bound and determined to find every one of them."
   _____

4. "So hopefully the slower pace in Alabama will help him by removing some of those temptations."
   _____

5. He thought I was the snitch but it was Joey.
   _____

6. By said, "Wait, let me dig this, you mean if I gotta go to the bathroom I gotta go outside into a little nasty thing like that? Ain't they got no sanitation laws down there?"
   _____

Prereading Vocabulary Worksheets *The Watsons Go to Birmingham–1963*

Chapters 9-10

Part II: Determining the Meaning:
Match the vocabulary words to their dictionary definitions.

_____ 1. jive   A. speed

_____ 2. bound   B. jazz or swing music

_____ 3. determined   C. firm; strong-minded

_____ 4. pace   D. someone who tells on others

_____ 5. snitch   E. certain to do something

_____ 6. sanitation   F. related to health and cleanliness

Prereading Vocabulary Worksheets *The Watsons Go to Birmingham–1963*

<u>Chapters 11-12</u>

Part I: Using Prior Knowledge and Contextual Clues
Below are the sentences in which the vocabulary words appear in the text. Read the sentence. Use any clues you can find in the sentence combined with your prior knowledge, and write what you think the underlined word means in the space provided.

1. "You talk about some <u>pathetic</u>, tortured-looking little faces. Eighteen hours in a car can age a kid forty years."
   _____

2. "Yeah, I swear I've been looking in the rear-view mirror and wondering where my babies were and where these three bad-<u>dispositioned</u>, sour-faced, middle-age midgets came from."
   _____

3. "But your sorry little <u>mugs</u> couldn't stop me either."
   _____

4. "In spite of all the cryin' and bawlin' and moanin' and <u>wailin'</u> and gnashin' of teeth I kept pushing on." (wailing)
   _____

5. "In spite of all the cryin' and bawlin' and moanin' and wailin' and <u>gnashin'</u> of teeth I kept pushing on." (gnashing)
   _____

6. I thought Grandma Sands would be bigger than Dad, I thought she'd be foaming at the mouth like she had <u>rabies</u>.
   _____

7. "Well, there ain't too many animals <u>wilier</u> or tougher than a old coon."
   _____

Prereading Vocabulary Worksheets *The Watsons Go to Birmingham–1963*

Chapters 11-12

Part II: Determining the Meaning:
Match the vocabulary words to their dictionary definitions.

_____ 1. pathetic   A. sad; causing feelings of pity

_____ 2. disposition   B. more clever at deceiving

_____ 3. mugs   C. mood; temperament

_____ 4. wailing   D. a disease of warm-blooded animals

_____ 5. gnashing   E. faces

_____ 6. rabies   F. clench; grind

_____ 7. wilier   G. crying

Prereading Vocabulary Worksheets *The Watsons Go to Birmingham–1963*

Chapters 13-14

Part I: Using Prior Knowledge and Contextual Clues
Below are the sentences in which the vocabulary words appear in the text. Read the sentence. Use any clues you can find in the sentence combined with your prior knowledge, and write what you think the underlined word means in the space provided.

1. "A couple of years ago Miss Thomas's little boy Jimmy got caught up in some kinda whirlpool there and they didn't find the poor soul's body for three days."
   _____

2. "WARNING! NO TRESSPASING! NO SWIMING! NO PUBLIC ENTREE! Signed Joe Collier." (trespassing)
   _____

3. "Naw, Joey, the Wool Pooh don't come on public beaches, he just grabs folks that are too stingy to let peons come on their land, like this Collier guy."
   _____

4. Something was wrong with him. If he was in Flint and you told him not to do something he'd go right out and do it, but now he was acting real dull and square.
   _____

5. Something was wrong with him. If he was in Flint and you told him not to do something he'd go right out and do it, but now he was acting real dull and square.
   _____

6. All the sound and light from Alabama disappeared because my eyes automatically shut and it seemed like my ears were stuffed with cotton.
   _____

7. Byron was shaking like he was getting electrocuted and crying like a baby and kissing the top of my head over and over!
   _____

8. I said, "Awww, man . . ." and tried to make him quit but all I could do was sit there too tired to do anything but let Daddy Cool nibble on the top of my head while he cried like a kindergarten baby.
   _____

Prereading Vocabulary Worksheets *The Watsons Go to Birmingham–1963*

Chapters 13-14

Part II: Determining the Meaning:
Match the vocabulary words to their dictionary definitions.

_____ 1. whirlpool   A. going to a place without permission

_____ 2. trespassing   B. not generous; not willing to share

_____ 3. stingy   C. take small, quick, playful bites

_____ 4. dull   D. a spiral current of water

_____ 5. square   E. out of touch

_____ 6. automatically   F. died by electrical shock

_____ 7. electrocuted   G. done without thought

_____ 8. nibble   H. not interesting; not exciting

Prereading Vocabulary Worksheets *The Watsons Go to Birmingham–1963*

Chapter 15

Part I: Using Prior Knowledge and Contextual Clues
Below are the sentences in which the vocabulary words appear in the text. Read the sentence. Use any clues you can find in the sentence combined with your prior knowledge, and write what you think the underlined word means in the space provided.

1. It was quiet and dark and still back there.
   _____

2. Whenever dogs survived the Word-Famous Watson Pet Hospital they always come out a lot friendlier.
   _____

3. I was getting too mature to play with toys anymore.
   _____

4. "Only thing that's gonna happen back there is that you gonna stunt your growth from being in a little ball all day."
   _____

5. Byron started throwing me curveballs.
   _____

6. Before he shut the door I could see that Momma and Dad and Joey were standing there in a little knot trying not to let me know they were eavesdropping.
   _____

7. If he'd ever had his ankle grabbed by it he'd know it was real, if he'd ever seen the way it was crouched down, crawling around in the dust and smoke of the church in Birmingham he'd know it wasn't some made up garbage . . . .
   _____

Prereading Vocabulary Worksheets *The Watsons Go to Birmingham–1963*

Chapter 15

Part II: Determining the Meaning:
Match the vocabulary words to their dictionary definitions.

_____ 1. still   A. stop; restrict

_____ 2. survived   B. listen in when the speaker does not know it

_____ 3. mature   C. grown-up; adult

_____ 4. stunt   D. distractions

_____ 5. curveballs   E. with no motion

_____ 6. eavesdropping F. in a posture low to the ground

_____ 7. crouched   G. stayed alive

ANSWER KEY PREREADING VOCABULARY WORKSHEETS
The Watsons Go to Birmingham - 1963

	Chapters 1-2	Chapters 3-4	Chapters 5-6	Chapters 7-8
1	D	B	C	D
2	I	G	F	F
3	A	D	E	H
4	F	F	B	J
5	J	A	D	A
6	B	C	A	B
7	H	E		E
8	E			I
9	C			G
10	G			C

	Chapters 9-10	Chapters 11-12	Chapters 13-14	Chapter 15
1	B	A	D	E
2	E	C	A	G
3	C	E	B	C
4	A	G	H	A
5	D	F	E	D
6	F	D	G	B
7		B	F	F
8			C	
9				
10				

DAILY LESSON PLANS

LESSON ONE

Objectives
1. To introduce the *The Watsons Go to Birmingham–1963* unit
2. To relate prior knowledge to the new material
3. To distribute books, study guides and other related materials
4. To become acquainted with the Nonfiction reading assignment

Activity #1
Show students some pictures of typical scenes of the United States around the year 1963. Include pictures that show the houses, automobiles, hairstyles, and roadways. Make sure to have a distribution of scenes from across the country, including Michigan and Alabama. If possible, show pictures that depict the racial discrimination of the times, including pictures of signs that say, "Whites Only," "Coloreds Only," and so forth. Explain that this book is about a black family and events that happened in their lives in the year 1963. It is written in first person from the point of view of Kenny, the middle child of three children. The story line includes some real and some fictitious events. Discuss with students why an author might want to write in this way. Ask students how they think they will benefit from reading the book.

Activity #2
Ask students to tell you what they know about the United States in 1963, and especially about Birmingham, Alabama. Do a group KWL with students (included in this Lit Plan.) Write any information the students know in the K column (What I Know). Ask students what they want to find out and write those questions in the W column (What I Want to Find Out.) Keep the KWL sheet and refer back to it as students read the book. After reading the book, work with the group to complete the L column (What I Learned.)

Activity #3
Distribute books, study guides, and reading assignments. Explain in detail how students are to use these materials.
Study Guides Students should preview the study guide questions before each reading assignment to get a feeling for what events and ideas are important in that section. After reading the section, students will (as a class or individually) answer the question to review the important events and ideas from that section of the book. Students should keep the study guides as study materials for the unit test.

Daily Lesson Plans *The Watsons Go to Birmingham–1963*

LESSON ONE, continued

Reading/Writing Assignment Sheet You (the teachers) need to fill in the reading and writing assignment sheet to let students know when their reading has to be completed. You can either write the assignment sheet on a side blackboard or bulletin board and leave it there for students to see each day, or you can duplicate copies for each student to have. In either case, you should advise students to become very familiar with the reading assignments so they know what is expected of them.

Unit Outline You may find it helpful to distribute copies of the Unit Outline to your students so they can keep track of upcoming lessons and assignments. You may also want to post a copy of the Unit Outline on a bulletin board and cross off each lesson as you complete it.

Extra Activities Center The Extra Activities Packet portion of this unit contains suggestions for a library of related books and articles in your classroom as well as crossword and word search puzzles. Make an extra activities center in your classroom where you will keep these materials for students to use. Bring the books and articles in from the library and keep several copies of the puzzles on hand. Explain to students that these materials are available for students to use when they finish reading assignments or other class work early.

Books Each school has its own rules and regulations regarding student use of schoolbooks. Advise students of the procedures that are normal for your school.

Notebook or Unit Folder You may want the students to keep all of their worksheets, notes, and other papers for the unit together in a binder or notebook. During the first class meeting, tell them how you want them to arrange the folder. Make divider pages for vocabulary worksheets, Prereading study guide questions, review activities, notes, and tests. You may want to give a grade for accuracy in keeping the folder.

Activity #4
Distribute copies of the Nonfiction Assignment Sheet and go over it in detail with the students. Explain to students that they each are to read at least one nonfiction piece at some time during the unit. This could be a book, a magazine article, or information from an encyclopedia or the Internet. Students will fill out a Nonfiction Assignment Sheet after completing the reading to help you (the teacher) evaluate their reading experiences and to help the students think about and evaluate their own reading. Encourage students to read about topics that are related to the theme of the novel.

KWL
The Watsons Go to Birmingham–1963

Directions: Before reading, think about what you already know about *The Watsons Go to Birmingham–1963* and /or Christopher Paul Curtis. Write the information in the **K** column. Think about what you would like to find out from reading the book. Write your questions in the **W** column. After you have read the book, use the **L** column to write the answers to your questions from the W column, and anything else you remember from the book.

K (What I Know)	W (What I Want to Know)	L (What I Learned)

NONFICTION ASSIGNMENT SHEET *The Watsons Go to Birmingham–1963*
(To be completed after reading the required nonfiction article.)

Name _____ Date _____ Class _____

Title of Nonfiction Read _____

Written by _____ Publication Date _____

Web Site Address (if applicable) _____

I. Factual Summary: Write a summary of the piece you read.

II. Vocabulary:
   1. Which vocabulary words were difficult?

   2. What did you do to help yourself understand the words?

III. Interpretation: What was the main point the author wanted you to get from reading his/her work?

IV. Criticism:
   1. Which points of the piece did you agree with or find easy to believe? Why?

   2. With which points of the piece did you disagree or find difficult to believe? Why?

V. Personal Response:
   1. What did you think about this piece?

   2. How does this piece help you understand the novel *The Watsons Go to Birmingham–1963*?

LESSON TWO

Objectives
1. To do the prereading work for Chapters 1-2
2. To read Chapters 1-2
3. To review the main ideas and events from Chapters 1-2

Activity #1
Show students how to preview the study questions and do the vocabulary work for Chapters 1-2. Encourage students to take notes as they read. If students own their books, encourage them to use highlighters or colored pens to mark important passages and the answers to the study guide questions.

Activity #2
Read Chapter 1 aloud to students to set the mood for the novel. Then have students read chapter 2 aloud. Either call on students or ask for volunteers, whichever works best with your class. Be sure to give students who need practice reading orally the opportunity to do so, even if it slows down the reading schedule a little. If you have not given students a grade for oral reading this quarter, during the reading of this novel would be a good time to grade them. Be sure to let them know that they will be evaluated and tell them the criteria you will use.

Activity #3
Give students time to answer the study guide questions from Chapters 1-2 and then discuss the answers in detail. Write the answers on the board or overhead projector film so students can have the correct answers for study purposes.

Note: It is a good practice in public speaking and leadership skills for individual students to take charge of leading the discussion of the study questions. Perhaps a different student could go to the front of the class and lead the discussion each day that the study questions are discussed during the unit.

LESSON THREE

Objectives
1. To do the prereading work for Chapters 3-4
2. To read Chapters 3-4
3. To review the main ideas and events from Chapters 3-4
4. To practice reading orally
5. To give the teacher the opportunity to evaluate students' reading skills

Activity #1
Give students about ten or fifteen minutes to complete the Prereading vocabulary worksheet and preview the study guide questions for Chapters 3-4.

Activity #2
Tell students their oral reading ability will be evaluated. Show them copies of the Oral Reading Evaluation form and discuss it. Model correct intonation and expression by reading the first few paragraphs of Chapter 3 aloud.

Activity #3
Call on individual students to read a few paragraphs aloud. Encourage the other students to follow along in their books. If you have a student who is unwilling or unable to read aloud in front of the group, make arrangements to do his or her evaluation privately at another time. Mark the oral reading evaluation forms as the students read. If all students have read orally before the chapters have been completed, assign the remainder of the text as individual silent reading.

Activity #4
Write the study questions on the board or on a piece of chart paper. Work with the whole class to answer the questions.

ORAL READING EVALUATION *The Watsons Go to Birmingham–1963*

Name _____ Class _____ Date _____

SKILL	EXCELLENT	GOOD	AVERAGE	FAIR	POOR
FLUENCY	5	4	3	2	1
CLARITY	5	4	3	2	1
AUDIBILITY	5	4	3	2	1
PRONUNCIATION	5	4	3	2	1
_____	5	4	3	2	1
_____	5	4	3	2	1
TOTAL GRADE	5	4	3	2	1

COMMENTS:

LESSON FOUR

Objectives
1. To review the main events and ideas in Chapters 3-4
2. To begin to identify examples of character traits

Activity #1
Have partners answer the study guide questions and review their prereading vocabulary worksheets. Go over the answers with the class. Then have partners write a few additional questions about the chapters. Have each pair read their questions aloud to the class and call on other students to answer.

Activity #2 Minilesson: Character Traits
Explain that in a story such as *The Watsons Go to Birmingham–1963* the author acquaints the readers with the characters by describing traits such as physical attributes, thoughts, and feelings. The author develops these traits in the characters by showing and telling what the characters say, do, and think. The author has given more details about some characters than about other characters. Since the story is written in the first person and by Kenny, one of the characters, is the narrator, all of the information about the other characters is described through Kenny's perspective. The reader's information is limited to what Kenny observes about the other characters' actions and what he knows about their thoughts and feelings. The reader will have to make some inferences and draw conclusions about many of the character traits. Remind students that this book is a fiction story that puts the characters in some real-life historical events. Through the characters we can see how people might have responded to these events.

Have students look for the character traits of both Kenny and Byron as they read. Distribute copies of the Character Traits Chart (included.) Ask students to fill in what they have learned about Kenny and Byron so far. Tell them they should continue to be aware of the character traits of both characters as they read, and that they will continue the discussion and complete more of the character chart during Lesson 15. As an extension, students can copy the Character Traits Chart and use it to write about other characters, such as Joey, Momma, Dad, or Grandma Sands.

CHARACTER TRAITS CHART
The Watsons Go to Birmingham–1963

Directions: Fill in the charts for Byron and Kenny with examples from the novel.

Byron's Character Traits	Words, Thoughts, or Actions That Illustrate the Trait

Kenny's Character Traits	Words, Thoughts, or Actions That Illustrate the Trait

LESSON FIVE

Objectives
    1. To do the prereading work for Chapters 5-6
    2. To read Chapters 5-6
    3. To review the main ideas and events from Chapters 5-6
    4. To become acquainted with Writing Assignment #1

Activity #1
    Have students complete the prereading work for the chapters individually and then check their answers in small groups.

Activity #2
    Have students stay in the same small groups and read the chapters aloud together. Students can take turns reading a page or two, or take the roles of the characters and a narrator and read the chapters.

Activity #3
    Keeping the same small groups, have students divide up the study guide questions and answer them. Then have students present their answers to the group. Remind students to write down the answers from other group members so they have them available to use for later test preparation.

Activity #4
    Distribute Writing Assignment #1 and discuss the directions in detail. Allow students the remainder of the class period to work on this assignment. Give students an additional two or three class periods to complete the assignment if necessary.

Distribute copies of the Writing Evaluation Form (included in this Lit Plan.) Explain to students that during Lesson Nine you will be holding individual writing conferences about this writing assignment. Make sure they are familiar with the criteria on the Writing Evaluation Form.

WRITING ASSIGNMENT #1 *The Watsons Go to Birmingham–1963*
Writing to Persuade

PROMPT
Throughout the first six chapters Kenny gives several examples of Byron's disobedience and misbehavior. So far, nothing that his parents have said has motivated Byron to change his behavior.

Take the point of view of someone outside of the immediate family, perhaps a friend or even a social worker or counselor. You are writing an email to Byron asking him to change his behavior and stop doing the mean and disobedient things he does.

PREWRITING
Skim the first six chapters of the book and make a list of the examples of Byron's misbehavior. (If your teacher approves, you may want to read ahead the next several chapters to find more examples of Byron's troublesome deeds.) Include details about what he did, who or what his target was, and how his behavior was different from what he had been told to do. Next to each example write how you think his behavior should change and why. Then rank the misdeeds in order of severity, in order from most to least disruptive.

Remember that a persuasion piece can and should include your reasons for your request. The reasons should be backed up with or examples from the story.

DRAFTING
Make an introductory statement in which you describe the problem. Next state your request.

Then use one paragraph for each of the reasons that you think Byron's behavior should change. Use the supporting statements for each reason.

Summarize your request and respectfully ask Byron to send you a reply email by a certain date, perhaps a week after receiving your email.

PEER EDITING
When you finish the rough draft of your persuasive piece, ask another student to read it. After reading your rough draft, the student should tell you what he/she liked best about your work, which parts were difficult to understand, and ways in which your work could be improved. Your reader should also be able to summarize your opinion about Byron's behavior and what you want him to do about it based on your text. Reread your text considering your critic's comments, and make the revisions you think are necessary.

PROOFREADING/EDITING
Do a final proofreading of your persuasive piece, double checking your grammar, spelling, organization, and the clarity of your ideas.

FINAL DRAFT
Follow your teacher's guidance for completing the final draft of your paper.

WRITING EVALUATION FORM *The Watsons Go to Birmingham–1963*

Name _____ Date _____ Class _____

Writing Assignment # _____

Circle One for Each Item:

Composition	Excellent	Good	Fair	Poor
Style	Excellent	Good	Fair	Poor
Grammar	Excellent	Good	Fair	Poor
Spelling	Excellent	Good	Fair	Poor
Punctuation	Excellent	Good	Fair	Poor
Legibility	Excellent	Good	Fair	Poor

Strengths:

Weaknesses:

Comments/Suggestions:

LESSON SIX

Objectives
1. To complete the prereading work for Chapters 7-8
2. To read Chapters 7-8
3. To review the main ideas and events in Chapters 7-8

Activity #1
Give students about fifteen minutes to do the prereading and vocabulary work for Chapters 7-8.

Activity #2
Give students most of the remainder of the period to silently read Chapters 7-8.

Activity #3
Allow about fifteen minutes at the end of the class period to go over the study questions together. Tell students they will have a quiz on Chapters 1-8 during the next class period. Give students time to go through their study guides and notes to see if they are missing any information. Provide assistance as necessary.

LESSON SEVEN

Objectives
    1. To demonstrate understanding of the main ideas and events in Chapters 1-8
    2. To participate in a writing conference with the teacher
    3. To revise Writing Assignment #1 based on the teacher's suggestions
    4. To complete the prereading work for Chapters 9-10
    5. To read Chapters 9-10

Activity #1

Quiz-Distribute quizzes (multiple choice study questions for Chapters 1-8) and give students about twenty minutes to complete them. Correct and grade the papers as a class. You may want to have students exchange papers or allow them to correct their own work. As an extra credit assignment, have students find the correct answers to any questions they missed and rewrite any "false" answers to be true. Collect the quizzes for recording the grades.

Activity #2

Call students individually to your desk or some other private area of the classroom. Discuss their papers from Writing Assignment #1. Use the completed Writing Evaluation form as a basis for your critique.

Activity #3

Students should use the class time when they are not in conference with you to do any of the following: work on their nonfiction reading assignment; revise Writing Assignment #1; complete the prereading work for Chapters 9-10; read those chapters; work on the Character Traits Charts; review the study guide questions and answers and prereading vocabulary worksheets they have completed so far.

LESSON EIGHT

Objectives
    1. To review the main ideas and events in Chapters 9-10
    2. To identify and discuss elements of the setting in the book

Activity #1

Have students sit in small groups to answer the study guide questions. Tell each group to choose a spokesperson. Discuss the answers to the study guide questions with the class, having each spokesperson respond for their group.

Activity #2 Minilesson: Setting

Explain to students that the setting includes the time and place of a story. Knowing the time and place will help them understand the story because they will understand why characters do certain things, why events happen, and why problems occur. The setting helps the readers get a visual image of a place and a time. Remind students that all or part of the setting may change during the course of a story. For example, characters may travel to another place, or a story may take place over an extended period of time.

Tell students that the setting is more important in some stories than in others. The setting is very important in *The Watsons Go to Birmingham–1963*. That is evident since the name of a place is in the title of the story, as is a specific date. The setting can support the author's purpose for writing the story.

Work with students to begin filling out the Setting Graphic Organizer (included.) Reread Chapter 1 with students. Point out that they can infer an approximate month and location in the first paragraph because the narrator says it is a cold Saturday. Ask students where the story might take place and which month it might be. Continue reading and find more details about the setting.

Tell students to continue taking notes on the organizer as they read. They will review the completed organizer in Lesson 15. At this time, discuss with students how the setting supports the author's purpose for writing the story.

SETTING GRAPHIC ORGANIZER

Directions: Fill in details about the setting of *The Watsons Go to Birmingham–1963*.

Chapter	Details About the Time	Details About the Place

Draw your impression of the setting:

LESSON NINE

Objectives
    To write to inform

Activity # 1
    Distribute Writing Assignment # 2 and discuss the directions in detail. Allow the remaining class time for students to work on the assignment. Give students an additional two or three class periods to complete the assignment if necessary.

LESSON TEN

Objectives
    1. To complete the prereading work for Chapters 11-12
    2. To read Chapters 11-12

Activity #1
    Give students ten or fifteen minutes to complete the prereading work for the chapters.

Activity #2:
    Have students read the chapters independently. If they finish reading and still have class time left, they can start answering the study guide questions or work on Writing Assignment #2. Tell them the study guide questions will be due at the next class period.

WRITING ASSIGNMENT #2 *The Watsons Go to Birmingham–1963*
Writing to Inform

PROMPT
In Chapter 8 you read that Momma was writing things down in a notebook. In Chapter 9 you read more details about the notebook. Now you will create a notebook for an automobile trip of your own.

PREWRITING
Choose a destination and the amount of time the trip will take. Make a list of the categories you will include in your notebook. Your categories will vary depending on other circumstances, such as who will be with you on the trip, and whether you plan to drive straight through or stop and do some sightseeing.

Use a roadmap to plan stops for your trip. You may also want to consult tour guidebooks from the library or Internet Web sites for information about places to visit. You will also find information about hotel prices, road tolls, and other expenses.

DRAFTING
Make an outline for your notebook. Decide how many chapters you want and an approximate number of pages for each chapter. Use one chapter for each category, such as meals, hotels, etc. Create a Table of Contents with interesting chapter titles. Go back after you finish and put in the page numbers.

Write the text for each chapter. Include illustrations, maps, or other visuals as necessary. Use lined notebook or blank paper, or a spiral copybook, whichever you think works best. Or, you may want to compose your text on the computer and print it out.

Think of a title and put it on the cover. Add an illustration if you like. Remember that this is a draft, so do not bind your work into a permanent notebook yet.

PEER EDITING
When you finish the rough draft of your notebook, ask another student to read it. After reading your rough draft, the student should tell you what he/she liked best about your work, which parts were difficult to understand, and ways in which your notebook could be improved. Reread your text considering your critic's comments, and make the revisions you think are necessary.

PROOFREADING/EDITING
Do a final proofreading of your notebook, double checking your grammar, spelling, organization, and the clarity of your ideas.

FINAL DRAFT
Follow your teacher's guidance for completing the final draft of your notebook.

LESSON ELEVEN

Objectives
    1. To review the main ideas and events in Chapters 11-12
    2. To complete the prereading work for Chapters 13-14
    3. To read Chapters 13-14

Activity #1

    Have students write the letters A, B, C, D on strips of paper. Write the multiple choice questions for Chapters 11-12 on chart paper, or make a transparency of the pages and show them on the overhead projector. Ask volunteers to read aloud the questions and answer choices. Tell students to hold up the paper strip that has the letter for their answer choice.

Activity #2

    Give students about ten or fifteen minutes to complete the prereading work for Chapters 13-14.

Activity #3

    Have students read Chapters 13-14 silently, or allow them to quietly read aloud with a partner. Tell them the answers to the study guide questions will be due at the next class period.

LESSON TWELVE

Objectives
    1. To review the main ideas and events in Chapters 13-14
    2. To complete the prereading work for Chapter 15
    3. To make predictions about how the novel will end
    4. To read Chapter 15 and the Epilogue

Activity #1
    Review the study guide questions from Chapters 13-14 with students. Then invite students to ask additional questions and have other students answer them.

Activity #2
    Divide the class into small groups to do the prereading work for Chapter 15. (There is no prereading work for the Epilogue.) Have each group decide how they want to approach the work. They may want to assign a few vocabulary words to each group member and have each member teach those words to the rest of the class. Or, they may have each member work independently and then gather as a group to go over the vocabulary words.

Activity #3
    Have students sit with the groups they formed for Activity #2. Before students read the study guide questions or the chapter, have them write down a prediction about how they think the story will end. Allow about ten minutes for students to discuss their predictions. Ask students to hold onto the papers where they wrote their predictions until they have finished reading the last chapter.
    Tell each group to choose a way to read Chapter 15 and the Epilogue. They may each read a page, ask one group member to read the whole chapter, or take the roles of the characters and a narrator. If they have time they can begin answering the study guide questions, which will be due for the next class session.

LESSON THIRTEEN

Objectives
1. To discuss predictions about the end of the story
2. To review the main ideas and events in Chapter 15
3. To identify and understand the mood of the story

Activity #1
   Ask students to get out their predictions again. Ask for a show of hands for the number of students who correctly predicted the ending. Invite students to explain what led them to make the predictions that they made.

Activity #2
   Have partners work together to prepare an oral answer to one of the study guide questions and present it to the class. Tell them they can either read the answer, dramatize it, or create a rap or poem to explain the answer.

Activity #3: Minilesson: Mood
   Explain to students that the mood is the feeling or atmosphere the author establishes for the story. The author gives the story a certain mood to create emotions in the reader. The author may use certain words and descriptive details to create a mood. There may be one mood throughout an entire story or there may be several shifts of mood throughout the story. The shifts occur to show how a character or a situation has changed. Readers who can identify the mood will usually understand the story better and appreciate the author's craft.
   Skim through the chapters and discuss with students what the mood is in each chapter. Have them identify words and descriptive details and write them on the board. Prompt students to use words such as *happy, carefree, loving, serious*, and *sad* as they describe the mood. Point out the marked change in mood before and after Chapter 14, which describes the bombing.
   As an extension, ask small groups of students to choose a song or an instrumental melody that they feel depicts the mood of one chapter. Play these for the class and discuss differences in opinion.

LESSON FOURTEEN

Objectives
To discuss *The Watsons Go to Birmingham–1963* at the interpretive and critical levels

Activity # 1
　　Use the Extra Writing Assignments/Discussions Questions as a springboard for discussing the novel in more depth. Either write answers to the questions on the board or simply have students take notes during the discussion.
　　NOTE: This is a good time to combine activities to have students practice note-taking skills. If time permits (or if you can make time), allow students to just take notes during the discussion. You should take notes answering the questions on an overhead projector transparency during the discussion, as if you were answering the questions on the board for students to copy. Leave the projector off during the discussion. When the discussion is complete, go back, turn on the projector and briefly review the ideas students should have written into their notes. Allow time for students to fix their notes so they have all the information you want them to have.
　　If there is extra time, encourage students to ask additional questions.

LESSON FIFTEEN

Objectives
　　1. To discuss selected quotations from the book
　　2. To discuss the completed graphic organizers

Activity # 1
　　Read the quotations with students. First ask them to give details from memory about the scene in the book from which the quote came. Then have students check in the book to verify the details. Discuss the importance of the quote.
　　Challenge students to memorize and recite one or more of the quotations.

Activity # 2
　　Go over the completed Character Traits Chart and Setting Chart with students. Allow time for students to ask questions and make any necessary corrections. Remind students to keep these charts and use them as study aids when they prepare for their test.
　　You may want to post correctly completed copies of the charts on a bulletin board and/or the class Web site for future reference.

EXTRA WRITING ASSIGNMENTS / DISCUSSION QUESTIONS
The Watsons Go to Birmingham–1963

Interpretive
1. Explain the significance of the title of the novel.
2. Explain the significance of each chapter title of the novel.
3. Plot the growth of Kenny and of Byron as a character throughout the novel.
4. What are the main conflicts in the novel? How are they resolved?
5. How important is the setting to the story?
6. Why do you think the family left Birmingham so quickly?
7. Discuss the changes in Bryon over the course of the novel.
8. Who is the main character? How is this shown in the novel?
9. At the end of Chapter 14, Kenny says he "saw his socks flying over the Alabama mud." What is he describing here?

Critical
10. What is the point of view of the novel? How does it affect your understanding of the story? How would the story be different if it were written from the point of view of another character or from a third person omniscient narrator?
11. Is the story of *The Watsons Go to Birmingham–1963* believable? Explain why or why not. Tell which parts are believable and which are not.
12. Are the characters in *The Watsons Go to Birmingham–1963* stereotypes? If so, explain the usefulness of employing stereotypes in the story. If they are not, explain how they merit individuality.
13. Discuss the imagery used in the book. How vivid is it? How effective is it?
14. Describe Christopher Paul Curtis's writing style. Explain why you do or do not like it.
15. How effective is the use of dialect in the story?
16. The mood changes dramatically in the last few chapters. How did you feel when the mood shifted?
17. The title of the novel is also the title of Momma's notebook. However, the notebook and trip are not mentioned until Chapter 8, which is halfway through the book. How effective was this strategy?
18. How effective were the parents in dealing with the following situations: behavior problems with Byron, emotional difficulties with Kenny, and emotional difficulties with Joey after the bombing? If you were the author, how would you have portrayed the parents?

Personal Response
19. Did you enjoy reading *The Watsons Go to Birmingham–1963?* Explain why or why not.
20. *The Watsons Go to Birmingham–1963* has several difficult or tragic events. Which was the most serious or moving, and why?
21. Which of the characters did you like and why? Was there a character you disliked? Why?

Extra Writing Assignments / Discussion Questions *The Watsons Go to Birmingham–1963*

Personal Response, continued

22. Did you enjoy the humor in the story? Why or why not?
23. Which scene or event in the book did you like most? Why?
24. The author incorporated a real event, the church bombing, into a fictional story. How effective was this device? Did it add to or take away from your enjoyment of the story?
25. Did Kenny's experiences change the way you look at yourself? How?
26. Did Byron's experiences change the way you look at yourself? How?
27. Would you recommend this book to another student? Why or why not?
28. If you could change one thing about the book, what would it be? Why?
28. Have you read any other stories similar to *The Watsons Go to Birmingham–1963*? If so, tell about them.
30. What questions would you like to ask the author?

QUOTATIONS
The Watsons Go to Birmingham–1963.

Discuss the significance of the following quotations:

1. "Kids," Dad said, "I almost wasn't your father. You guys came real close to having a clown for a daddy named Hambone Henderson . . . ." (Ch. 1)

2. "Oh, yeah," Dad interrupted. "They're a laugh a minute down there. Let's see, where was that 'Coloreds Only' bathroom downtown?" (Ch. 1)

3. "Oh, Mom-ma! Hel' me! Geh me offa 'ere!" (Ch. 1)

4. "I want you to carefully note how advanced this second-grade student is, and I particularly want you to be aware of the effect his skills have upon you. I want you to be aware that some of our kids read at miraculous levels." (Ch. 2)

5. "Naw, man, keep your head straight and look at me sideways." I did it. "See? You ain't cockeyed no more, your eyes is straight as a arrow now!" (Ch. 2)

6. "Give my regards to Clark, Poindexter." (Ch. 2)

7. "Don't you pay no mind to them little fools, they ain't happy lest they draggin' someone down." Y'all just sit next to Poindexter, he don't bother no one." (Ch. 2)

8. "Kenny? I thought they said your name was Poindexter." (Ch. 3)

9. "I thought you was my friend. I didn't think you was like all them other people." I thought you was different." (Ch. 3)

10. "Here come some of them Weird Watsons doing their Mummy imitations." (Ch. 4)

11. "If you ever, ever . . . play with–no, if you ever even look at . . . another match in this house . . . I will personally, by myself . . . I will burn not just one finger, I will burn your entire hand, then send you to juvenile home!" (Ch. 5)

12. "I can't believe it. You really gonna start serving welfare food in this house? You really gonna make me go embarrass myself by signing a welfare list for some groceries like a blanged peon?" (Ch. 6)

13. "Get the hell out of here, what you starin' at? Them apples got me sick, you little cross-eyed punk! Get out of here." (Ch. 6)

14. "You've gone and done it, haven't you? (Ch. 7)

Daily Lesson Plans *The Watsons Go to Birmingham–1963*
Quotations, continued

15. "This is it, By. You're old enough now and you've been told enough, this time something's going to be done." (Ch. 7)

16. "It's a smelly green pine tree!" (Ch. 8)

17. "There's just too much, Byron. We can't have all this nonsense going on." (Ch. 8)

18. "Let him go, Daniel, he better get as much of that nonsense out of his system as he can. Grandma Sands won't be putting up with any of that mess." (Ch. 9)

19. "Well, a lot of times that's going to be the way of the world for you kids. Byron is getting old enough to have to understand that his time for playing is running out fast, he's got to realize the world doesn't have a lot of jokes waiting for him. He's got to be ready. (Ch. 9)

20. "Well, that's what being a grown-up is like. At first it's scary but then before you realize, with a lot of practice, you have it under control. Hopefully you'll have lots of time to practice being grown-up before you actually have to do it." (Ch. 9)

21. "But Mommy, it's white. (Ch. 9)

22. " 'Cuz, boy, this he-uh is the deep South you-all is gonna be drivin' thoo. Y'all colored folks cain't be jes' pullin' up tuh any ol' way-uh an be 'spectin' tuh get no room uh no food, yuh heah, boy? I said yuh heah what I'm sayin', boy?" (Ch. 9)

23. "I think we've got our fingers in God's beard and as we drive along we're tickling him." (Ch. 10)

24. "You grew up to be a fine-lookin' boy. You was so puny when you was born you nearly worried us crazy. Got strong, too." (Ch. 11)

25. "What you expect? You seen her. That bird's as old as dirt. She's so old I bet she used to step over dinosaur turds. I ain't gonna have her death on my hands." (Ch. 11)

26. "If Kenny wants to take his stupid little behind down there and get snatched, let him." (Ch. 13)

27. "Hmm, must have been a sonic boom." (Ch. 14)

28. "Where'd you go? How'd you get back here so fast? How come you changed your clothes?" (Ch. 14)

Daily Lesson Plans *The Watsons Go to Birmingham–1963*
Quotations, continued

29. "Whose shoe is that?" (Ch. 14)

30. "He's been disappearing, Daniel. Hours go by and I don't know where he is." (Ch. 15)

31. "Shut up and cry if you want to." (Ch. 15)

32. "Why would they want to do that, Byron? Why would they hurt some little kids like that?" (Ch. 15)

33. "You think I don't know you waiting for some stupid magic powers or genies or a angel to make you feel better? Dig this: You can wait behind that couch for the rest of your life and ain't no magic powers gonna come back there and make you feel nothing. Only thing that's gonna happen back there is that you gonna stunt your growth from being a little ball all day." (Ch. 15)

34. "Kenny, things ain't ever going to be fair. How's it fair that two grown men could hate Negroes so much that they'd kill some kids just to stop them from gong to school? How's it fair that even though the cops down there might know who did it nothing will probably ever happen to those men? It ain't. But you just gotta understand that's the way it is and keep on steppin'." (Ch. 15)

LESSON SIXTEEN

Objectives
 To write to express a personal opinion

Activity #1
 Write the word opinion on the board and ask students what it means. Invite them to give their opinions on topics such as what should be served for lunch in the school cafeteria, if the school should have a dress code, which football team should win a championship, and what kind of music they like. Ask other students to agree or disagree and state their reasons. Make the point that all people have opinions. A person expressing an opinion should be able to back it up with facts and reasons why he/she has the opinion.

Activity #2
 Distribute copies of Writing Assignment #3. Go over the assignment in detail with the students. Tell them they will have the remainder of the class period to work on the assignment. Explain that this assignment is brief and does not require any research, so they should be able to complete it in class or by the next class period at the latest.
 You may want to have pairs of students deliver their personal opinion papers in the form of a conversation with Kenny.

WRITING ASSIGNMENT #3 *The Watsons Go to Birmingham–1963*
Personal Opinion

PROMPT
In Chapter 15, Kenny says Byron was "wrong about there not being anything like magic powers or genies or angels. Maybe those weren't the things that could make a run-over dog walk without wobbling but they were out there." He goes on to say what he thinks some magic powers are. You are talking to Kenny and you share your opinion about magical powers.

PREWRITING
Reread that section of Chapter 15. Then give your opinion on what Kenny thought about magic powers. Ask yourself how you feel about magical powers. Do you agree with the examples that Kenny gave? If you believe as he does, what examples would you give? If you disagree, what events in your life caused you to form that opinion? Make notes on paper to refer to later as you write.

DRAFTING
Since this writing assignment is meant to be spoken, your writing style can be more informal than usual. Explain your opinion in the first few sentences. Back up your opinion with personal experiences or facts. Explain why you agree or disagree with Kenny, but do so without criticizing or judging his opinion.

PEER EDITING
When you finish the rough draft of your opinion paper, ask another student to read it. After reading your rough draft, the student should tell you what he/she liked best about your work, which parts were difficult to understand, where you need more support for your opinion, and ways in which your opinion could be stated more clearly. Reread your opinion paper considering your critic's comments, and make the revisions you think are necessary.

PROOFREADING/EDITING
Do a final proofreading of your opinion paper, double checking your grammar, spelling, organization, and the clarity of your ideas.

FINAL DRAFT
Follow your teacher's guidance for making a final copy of your paper.

LESSON SEVENTEEN

Objective
To review all of the vocabulary work done in this unit

VOCABULARY REVIEW ACTIVITIES

1. Divide your class into two teams and have an old-fashioned spelling or definition bee.

2. Give individuals or groups of students a *The Watsons Go to Birmingham–1963* Vocabulary Word Search Puzzle with a word list. The person (group) to find all of the vocabulary words in the puzzle first wins.

3. Give students a *The Watsons Go to Birmingham–1963* Vocabulary Word Search Puzzle without the word list. The person or group to find the most vocabulary words in the puzzle wins.

4. Put a *The Watsons Go to Birmingham–1963* Vocabulary Crossword Puzzle onto a transparency on the overhead projector and do the puzzle together as a class.

5. Give students a *The Watsons Go to Birmingham–1963* Vocabulary Matching Worksheet to do.

6. Use words from the word jumble page and have students spell them correctly, then use them in original sentences.

7. Have students write a story in which they correctly use as many vocabulary words as possible. Have students read their compositions orally. Post the most original compositions on your bulletin board.

8. Have students work in teams and play charades with the vocabulary words.

9. Select a word of the day and encourage students to use it correctly in their writing and speaking vocabulary.

10. Have a contest to see which students can find the most vocabulary words used in other sources. You may want to have a bulletin board available so the students can write down their word, the sentence it was used in, and the source.

11. Assign a word to each student, or let them choose a word. Have them look up the origin of the word, the part of speech, definition, a synonym, and an antonym. Then have them write a sentence using the word. Have students present their information orally to the class.

LESSON EIGHTEEN

Objective
To review the main events and ideas of *The Watsons Go to Birmingham–1963*

Activity #1
Choose one of the review games/activities included in this packet and spend your class time as outlined there.

Activity #2
Remind students of the date of the unit test. Stress the review of the study guides and their class notes as a last minute, brush-up review.

REVIEW GAMES/ACTIVITIES *The Watsons Go to Birmingham–1963*

1. Ask the class to make up a unit test for *The Watsons Go to Birmingham–1963* (including a separate answer key). The test should have 4 sections: multiple choice, true/false, short answer, and essay. Students may use 1/2 period to make the test with a separate answer key and then swap papers and use the other 1/2 class period to take a test a classmate has devised. (open book) You may want to use the unit test included in this packet or take questions from the students' unit tests to formulate your own test.

2. Take 1/2 period for students to make up true and false questions (including the answers). Collect the papers, and divide the class into two teams. Draw a big tic-tac-toe board on the chalkboard. Make one team X and one team O. Ask questions to each side, giving each student one turn. If the question is answered correctly, that students' team's letter (X or O) is placed in the box. If the answer is incorrect, no mark is placed in the box. The object is to get three marks in a row like tic-tac-toe. You may want to keep track of the number of games won for each team.

3. Take 1/2 period for students to make up questions (true/false and short answer). Collect the questions. Divide the class into two teams. You'll alternate asking questions to individual members of teams A & B (like in a spelling bee). The question keeps going from A to B until it is correctly answered, then a new question is asked. A correct answer does not allow the team to get another question. Correct answers are +2 points; incorrect answers are -1 point.

4. Allow students time to quiz each other (in pairs or small groups) from their study guides and class notes.

5. Give students a *The Watsons Go to Birmingham–1963* crossword puzzle to complete.

Review Games/Activities Continued *The Watsons Go to Birmingham–1963*

7. Divide your class into two teams. Use the *The Watsons Go to Birmingham–1963* crossword clue words with their letters jumbled as a word list. Student 1 from Team A faces off against Student 1 from Team B. You write the first jumbled word on the board. The first student (1A or 1B) to unscramble the word wins the chance for his/her team to score points. If 1A wins the jumble, go to student 2A and give him/her a clue. He/she must give you the correct word which matches that clue. If he/she does, Team A scores a point, and you give student 3A a clue for which you expect another correct response. Continue giving Team A clues until some team member makes an incorrect response. An incorrect response sends the game back to the jumbled-word face off, this time with students 2A and 2B. Instead of repeating giving clues to the first few students of each team, continue with the student after the one who gave the last incorrect response on the team.

8. Take on the persona of "The Answer Person." Allow students to ask any question about the book. Answer the questions, or tell students where to look in the book to find the answer.

9. Students may enjoy playing charades with events from the story. Select a student to start. Give him/her a card with a scene or event from the story. Allow the players to use their books to find the scene being described. The first person to guess each charade performs the next one.

10. Play a categories-type quiz game. (A master is included in this Unit Plan). Make an overhead transparency of the categories form. Divide the class into teams of three or four players each. Have each team Choose a recorder and a banker. Choose a team to go first. That team will choose a category and point amount. Ask the question to the entire class.(Use the Study Guide Quiz and Vocabulary questions.) Give the teams one minute to discuss the answer and write it down. Walk around the room and check the answers. Each team that answers correctly receives the points. (Incorrect answers are not penalized; they just don't receive any points). Cross out that square on the playing board. Play continues until all squares have been used. The winning team is the one with the most points. You can assign bonus points to any square or squares you choose.

11. Have individual students draw scenes from the book. Display the scenes and have the rest of the class look in their books to find the chapter or section that is being depicted. The first student to find the correct scene then displays his or her picture. When the game is over, collect the pictures and put them in a binder for students to look at during their free time.

NOTE: If students do not need the extra review, omit this lesson and go on to the test.

QUIZ GAME *The Watsons Go to Birmingham–1963*

Chapters 1-3	Chapters 4-6	Chapters 7-9	Chapters 10-12	Chapters 13-15
100	**100**	**100**	**100**	**100**
200	**200**	**200**	**200**	**200**
300	**300**	**300**	**300**	**300**
400	**400**	**400**	**400**	**400**
500	**500**	**500**	**500**	**500**

LESSON NINETEEN

Objective
To test the students understanding of the main ideas, themes, and events in *The Watsons Go to Birmingham–1963*

Activity #1
Distribute *The Watsons Go to Birmingham–1963* tests. Discuss the directions in detail and allow students the entire class period to complete the test. If they finish this segment early, they may continue to work on their "take home" essays (Writing Assignment #3) until the end of the period.

Activity #2
Collect all test papers and assigned books prior to the end of the period.

NOTES ABOUT THE UNIT TESTS IN THIS UNIT:

There are 5 different unit tests which follow.

There are two short answer tests, which are based primarily on facts from the novel. The answer key for Short Answer Unit Test 1 follows the student test. The answer key for Short Answer Unit Test 2 follows the student version of Short Answer Unit Test 2.

There is one Advanced Short Answer Unit Test. It is based on the extra discussion questions. Use the matching key for Short Answer Unit Test 2 to check the matching section of the Advanced Short Answer Unit Test. There is no key for the short answer questions. The answers will be based on the discussions you have had during class.

There are two Multiple Choice Unit Tests. Following the two unit tests, you will find an answer sheet on which students should mark their answers. The same answer sheet should be used for both tests; however, students' answers will be different for each test. Following the students' answer sheet for the multiple choice tests you will find your two keys: one for Multiple-Choice Unit Test 1 and one for Multiple Choice Unit Test 2. If you follow the directions at the top of each of those pages, you should be able to overlay your answer key on the students' answer sheets and easily grade the papers.

Each of the short answer tests has a vocabulary section. You should choose 10 of the vocabulary words from this unit, read them orally and have the students write them down. Then, either have students write a definition or use the words in sentences. The second part of the vocabulary test is matching.

LESSON TWENTY

Objectives
    1. To widen the breadth of students' knowledge about the topics discussed or touched upon in *The Watsons Go to Birmingham–1963*
    2. To present the nonfiction assignments

Activity #1
    Ask each student to give a brief oral report about the nonfiction work he/she read for the nonfiction assignment. Your criteria for evaluating this report will vary depending on the level of your students. You may wish for students to give the complete report without using notes of any kind. Or you may want students to read directly from a written report. You may want to do something between these two options. Make students aware of your criteria in ample time for them to prepare their reports.
    Start with one student's report. After that, ask if anyone else in the class has read on a topic related to the first student's report. If no one has, choose another student at random. After each report, be sure to ask if anyone has a report related to the one just completed. That will help keep continuity during the discussion of the reports.

Activity #2
    Collect the students' written reports. Put them in a binder and have the binder available for students to read.

Activity #3
    If the class or school has a Web site, post the nonfiction reports there.

UNIT TESTS

SHORT ANSWER UNIT TEST 1 *The Watsons Go to Birmingham –1963*

I. Matching/Identification:
Directions: Place the letter of the matching definition on the blank line.

_____ 1. Kenny   A. little sister; left the bombed church
_____ 2. Joey   B. where grandmother lived
_____ 3. Byron   C. forced to play "Great Carp Escape"
_____ 4. Larry Dunn   D. helped Byron with his conk hairstyle
_____ 5. Rufus   E. narrator of story
_____ 6. Buphead   F. where family lived
_____ 7. LJ Jones   G. Rufus's brother; shot squirrels
_____ 8. Birmingham   H. stole narrator's toy dinosaurs
_____ 9. Flint   I. older brother; helped narrator at end of story
_____ 10. Cody   J. personal savior to story's narrator

II. Short Answer
Directions: Write a detailed answer for each question.

1. Dad talked with Kenny about the reasons they were sending Byron to Alabama. What did Dad tell Kenny?

2. What did Kenny expect Grandma Sands to look like? What did she really look like?

Short Answer Unit Test 1 *The Watsons Go to Birmingham –1963*

II. Short Answer, continued

3. Describe the game called "The Great Carp Escape." Explain who was playing it and why. Tell how Kenny felt about the game.

4. Describe what happened when Kenny went into the water at Collier's Landing. Include what happened before and after he went in the water.

5. Describe what Kenny did and saw when he got to the church.

6. What did Kenny think would happen when the teacher sat Rufus next to him in class? Was he right or wrong? Explain what happened.

Short Answer Unit Test 1 *The Watsons Go to Birmingham –1963*

7. What did Momma tell the boys to do when they went to Mitchell's store for some groceries? What did Byron think this meant, and how did he feel about it? Was Byron's assumption correct?

8. Describe the incident with Byron's hair. Tell what he did, why he did it, and who helped him. Tell what Momma said about it and what Dad did about it. Name the song Dad whistled while he took care of Byron's punishment.

9. What happened to Byron when he and Kenny were scraping the ice off the car windows? What did Kenny call Byron after that?

10. Summarize what happened when Bryon took Kenny into the bathroom after they had been back from Birmingham for a while.

Short Answer Unit Test 1 *The Watsons Go to Birmingham –1963*

III. Quotations

Directions: Identify the speaker and discuss the significance of each of the following quotations.

1. "Naw, man, keep your head straight and look at me sideways." I did it. "See? You ain't cockeyed no more, your eyes is straight as a arrow now!"

2. "Oh, yeah," ____ interrupted. "They're a laugh a minute down there. Let's see, where was that 'Coloreds Only' bathroom downtown?"

3. "I want you to carefully note how advanced this second-grade student is, and I particularly want you to be aware of the effect his skills have upon you. I want you to be aware that some of our kids read at miraculous levels."

4. "I thought you was my friend. I didn't think you was like all them other people. I thought you was different."

5. "It's a smelly green pine tree!"

Short Answer Unit Test 1 *The Watsons Go to Birmingham –1963*

III. Quotations, continued

6. "You grew up to be a fine-lookin' boy. You was so puny when you was born you nearly worried us crazy. Got strong, too."

7. "You think I don't know you waiting for some stupid magic powers or genies or a angel to make you feel better?"

8. "He's been disappearing. Hours go by and I don't know where he is."

9. "Get the hell out of here, what you starin' at? Them apples got me sick, you little cross-eyed punk! Get out of here."

10. If you ever, ever . . . play with–no, if you ever even look at . . . another match in this house . . . I will personally, by myself . . . I will burn not just one finger, I will burn your entire hand, then send you to juvenile home!"

Short Answer Unit Test 1 *The Watsons Go to Birmingham –1963*

IV: Essay

Describe the mood of the story. Explain when the mood changes, how it changes, and why. Include how you felt about the mood change and explain why.

Short Answer Unit Test 1 *The Watsons Go to Birmingham –1963*

V. Vocabulary Part 1
Directions: Listen to the vocabulary word and spell it. After you have spelled all the words, go back and write down the definitions.

WORD   DEFINITION

1. _____   _____

2. _____   _____

3. _____   _____

4. _____   _____

5. _____   _____

6. _____   _____

7. _____   _____

8. _____   _____

9. _____   _____

10. _____   _____

Vocabulary Part 2:
Directions: Place the letter of the matching definition on the blank line.

_____ 1. automatically   A. having greater age or higher rank
_____ 2. dispositioned   B. stop; restrict
_____ 3. emulate   C. not able to feel emotions
_____ 4. hostile   D. put up with
_____ 5. numb   E. more clever at deceiving
_____ 6. seniority   F. aid in the form of money and other benefits
_____ 7. stunt   G. done without thought
_____ 8. tolerate   H. full of hatred or anger
_____ 9. welfare   I. related to mood or temperament
_____ 10. wilier   J. try to be like someone else

ANSWER KEY SHORT ANSWER UNIT TEST 1
The Watsons Go to Birmingham –1963

I. Matching/Identification:

Directions: Place the letter of the matching definition on the blank line.

E	1. Kenny	A.	little sister; left the bombed church
A	2. Joey	B.	where grandmother lived
I	3. Byron	C.	forced to play "Great Carp Escape"
C	4. Larry Dunn	D.	helped Byron with his conk hair style
J	5. Rufus	E.	narrator of story
D	6. Buphead	F.	where family lived
H	7. LJ Jones	G.	Rufus's brother; shot squirrels
B	8. Birmingham	H.	stole narrator's toy dinosaurs
F	9. Flint	I.	older brother; helped narrator at end of story
G	10. Cody	J.	personal savior to story's narrator

II. Short Answer

Directions: Write a detailed answer for each question.

1. Dad talked with Kenny about the reasons they were sending Byron to Alabama. What did Dad tell Kenny?

   Dad told Kenny that Byron was learning things they didn't want him to learn, and he was not learning the things they wanted him to learn. They thought that spending some time in the South would open Byron's eyes to the way the world could be; that there were not a lot of jokes waiting for Byron when he got older.

2. What did Kenny expect Grandma Sands to look like? What did she really look like?

   He expected a troll. He thought she would be bigger than Dad and foaming at the mouth. Instead, she was a very small old woman who looked like a shrunken version of his mother.

3. Describe the game called "The Great Carp Escape." Explain who was playing it and why. Tell how Kenny felt about the game.

   Larry had stolen Kenny's good leather gloves. When Byron found out, he and Buphead got them back. They punished Larry by playing "The Great Carp Escape." This was a game where Byron made Larry act like a carp trying to get out of a net in the Flint River. Byron threw Larry against the chain link fence over and over. Kenny wished he had not told Byron about the problem with the gloves. He could not stand watching and left the schoolyard.

Answer Key Short Answer Unit Test 1 *The Watsons Go to Birmingham –1963*
Short Answer, continued

4. Describe what happened when Kenny went into the water at Collier's Landing. Include what happened before and after he went in the water.

    They were told to stay away from Collier's Landing because a little boy had got caught up in a whirlpool and drowned there. Kenny went to Collier's Landing anyway. Byron and Joey did not go with him. He waded out to catch a fish and he got caught in the whirlpool. Byron and Joey saved him. When Kenny was out of the water Byron kept repeating, "Kenny, Kenny" and kissing the top of Kenny's head.

5. Describe what Kenny did and saw when he got to the church.

    He went inside and saw smoke and dust. He saw a shiny black shoe under some concrete and pulled on it. Then he thought he saw the Wool Pooh again. He grabbed the shoe and left the church with it. Then he went back to Grandma Sands's house.

6. What did Kenny think would happen when the teacher sat Rufus next to him in class? Was he right or wrong? Explain what happened.

    He was upset. He thought that now he would get picked on even more, since they were both people who got teased anyway. He was wrong. The other kids left Kenny alone and started picking on Rufus.

7. What did Momma tell the boys to do when they went to Mitchell's store for some groceries? What did Byron think this meant, and how did he feel about it? Was Byron's assumption correct?

    Momma told Byron to sign for the groceries. He thought that meant they were on welfare. He was embarrassed to sign a welfare list like a peon. He made Kenny sign for the food. Byron's assumption was not correct. The family was not on welfare. Mr. Watson had arranged to pay the bill all at once.

8. Describe the incident with Byron's hair. Tell what he did, why he did it, and who helped him. Tell what Momma said about it and what Dad did about it. Name the song Dad whistled while he took care of Byron's punishment.

    Byron with Buphead's help got a conk, or process, which meant that he chemically straightened his hair. Momma sent Byron to his room and said that Byron would be at his father's mercy. Byron said he did it because he wanted a Mexican hairstyle. Dad shaved Byron's head bald while whistling, "Straighten Up and Fly Right."

9. What happened to Byron when he and Kenny were scraping the ice off the car windows? How was the problem solved? What did Kenny call Byron after that?

    Byron kissed his image in the side mirror and his lips froze to the mirror. Momma pulled Byron's lips off of the mirror. After that Kenny called him, "The Lipless Wonder."

Answer Key Short Answer Unit Test 1 *The Watsons Go to Birmingham –1963*

10. Summarize what happened when Bryon took Kenny into the bathroom after they had been back from Birmingham for a while.

    Byron took Kenny into the bathroom to show him a hair on his (Byron's) chin. When Kenny looked in the mirror and saw himself looking so sad he started crying. He asked Byron why the men would want to hurt kids by bombing the church. Kenny said he was ashamed because he left Joey in the church when he thought the Wool Pooh had her.

III. Quotations

Directions: Identify the speaker and discuss the significance of each of the following quotations.

1. "Naw, man, keep your head straight and look at me sideways." I did it. "See? You ain't cockeyed no more, your eyes is straight as a arrow now!"

    Byron gave these directions to Kenny. Kenny was cross-eyed and was embarrassed to look at people.

2. "Oh, yeah," ____ interrupted. "They're a laugh a minute down there. Let's see, where was that 'Coloreds Only' bathroom downtown?"

    Dad said this in response to Momma saying that Birmingham was a good place to live.

3. "I want you to carefully note how advanced this second-grade student is, and I particularly want you to be aware of the effect his skills have upon you. I want you to be aware that some of our kids read at miraculous levels."

    Kenny tells this flashback story about something that happened to him in second grade. His teacher, Miss Henry, used to take him to other rooms and have him read for the students. Once she took him to Byron's class and his teacher, Mr. Alums, delivered this speech to the class.

4. "I thought you was my friend. I didn't think you was like all them other people." I thought you was different."

    Rufus said this to Kenny. The other boys were teasing Rufus and Cody and Kenny joined in the laughter. Later when Kenny went to Rufus's house and asked him to play, this was Rufus's response.

5. "It's a smelly green pine tree!"

    Joey said this. Dad bought it for the car and asked Joey to put it on the car. Dad described it as "the pinnacle of Western Civilization" and "the ultimate in American knowledge."

6. "You grew up to be a fine-lookin' boy. You was so puny when you was born you nearly worried us crazy. Got strong, too."

    Grandma Sands said this to Byron when they arrived at her house in Birmingham.

Answer Key Short Answer Unit Test 1 *The Watsons Go to Birmingham –1963*

7. "You think I don't know you waiting for some stupid magic powers or genies or a angel to make you feel better?"
    Byron said this to Kenny when they were in the bathroom. They had returned from Birmingham and Kenny had been hiding behind the sofa. Byron got Kenny to go to the bathroom to look at a hair on his (Byron's chin) and Kenny started crying.

8. "He's been disappearing. Hours go by and I don't know where he is."
    Momma said this to Dad after they had returned from Birmingham. She was worried about Kenny.

9. "Get the hell out of here, what you starin' at? Them apples got me sick, you little cross-eyed punk! Get out of here."
    Byron said this to Kenny after Byron hit and killed the mourning dove. Kenny saw Byron getting sick.

10. If you ever, ever . . . play with–no, if you ever even look at . . . another match in this house . . . I will personally, by myself . . . I will burn not just one finger, I will burn your entire hand, then send you to juvenile home!"
    Momma said this to Byron after he had been caught lighting matches in the bathroom. He had been told several times not to do that.

IV: Essay
Describe the mood of the story. Explain when the mood changes, how it changes, and why. Include how you felt about the mood change and explain why.

(for teacher notes)

Short Answer Unit Test 1 Answer Key Continued *Watsons Go To Birmingham–1963*

V. Vocabulary Part 1

WORD	DEFINITION
1.	
2.	
3.	
4.	
5.	
6.	
7.	
8.	
9.	
10.	

Vocabulary Part 2: Place the letter of the matching definition on the blank line.

G   1. automatically   A. having greater age or higher rank
I   2. dispositioned   B. stop; restrict
J   3. emulate   C. not able to feel emotions
H   4. hostile   D. put up with
C   5. numb   E. more clever at deceiving
A   6. seniority   F. aid in the form of money and other benefits
B   7. stunt   G. done without thought
D   8. tolerate   H. full of hatred or anger
F   9. welfare   I. related to mood or temperament
E   10. wilier   J. try to be like someone else

SHORT ANSWER UNIT TEST 2 *The Watsons Go to Birmingham –1963*

I. Matching/Identification
Directions: Place the letter of the matching definition on the blank line.

_____ 1. squirrel   A. Dad did not keep his with the rest of the family

_____ 2. dove   B. pinnacle of Western Civilization"

_____ 3. toothbrush   C. Rufus and Cody ate this animal in stew back home

_____ 4. bathroom   D. record player: True-Tone AB-700 ___

_____ 5. mirror   E. family car: 1948 Plymouth _____

_____ 6. pine tree   F. "World Famous Watson Pet ____"

_____ 7. Ultra Glide   G. there was one for "Coloreds Only" in Birmingham

_____ 8. "Brown Bomber"   H. Byron killed and buried this animal

_____ 9. hospital   I. site of bombings

_____ 10. church   J. place on car where Byron's lips froze

II. Short Answer

1. What did Momma catch Byron doing in the bathroom and what did she say she would do to him? Was Momma successful in carrying out her threat? Explain why or why not.

2. What news did the parents tell the children while they were all sitting in the car listening to the records? What were their reasons for this news?

Short Answer Unit Test 2 *The Watsons Go to Birmingham –1963*

3. How did Kenny think of Rufus and why?

4. What fictional characters did Kenny use to describe how he expected the meeting between Grandma Sands and Byron to go? What characters did he use to describe how the meeting actually went? How did Kenny feel about the reality of the meeting?

5. Describe the conversation between Joey and Kenny back at Grandma Sands's house after Kenny came back from the church. What did Joey tell Kenny about her time in the church that morning?

6. Which one of the children were the parents the most worried about? Why?

Short Answer Unit Test 2 *The Watsons Go to Birmingham –1963*

7. Summarize what happened when Bryon took Kenny into the bathroom. What did Byron say Kenny should think about? How did Kenny feel at the end of the story?

8. What did Kenny think about making Byron spend a whole summer in the heat? How did Byron seem to be taking it?

9. What was the title of Momma's notebook? What was on the cover? What were the contents?

10. Why was Rufus upset with Kenny? What happened as a result? How did Kenny feel? How was the problem solved?

Short Answer Unit Test 2 *The Watsons Go to Birmingham –1963*

III. Quotations
Directions: Identify the speaker and discuss the significance of the following quotations.

1. "Oh, Mom-ma! Hel' me! Geh me offa 'ere!"

2. "Don't you pay no mind to them little fools, they ain't happy lest they draggin' someone down." Y'all just sit next to Poindexter, he don't bother no one."

3. "I can't believe it. You really gonna start serving welfare food in this house? You really gonna make me go embarrass myself by signing a welfare list for some groceries like a blanged peon?"

4. "Well, that's what being a grown-up is like. At first it's scary but then before you realize, with a lot of practice, you have it under control. Hopefully you'll have lots of time to practice being grown-up before you actually have to do it."

5. " 'Cuz, boy, this he-uh is the deep South you-all is gonna be drivin' thoo. Y'all colored folks cain't be jes' pullin' up tuh any ol' way-uh an be 'spectin' tuh get no room uh no food, yuh heah, boy? I said yuh heah what I'm sayin', boy?"

Short Answer Unit Test 2 *The Watsons Go to Birmingham –1963*

III. Quotations, continued

6. "What you expect? You seen her. That bird's as old as dirt. She's so old I bet she used to step over dinosaur turds. I ain't gonna have her death on my hands."

7. "If Kenny wants to take his stupid little behind down there and get snatched, let him."

8. "Shut up and cry if you want to."

9. "Kenny, things ain't ever going to be fair. How's it fair that two grown men could hate Negroes so much that they'd kill some kids just to stop them from going to school? How's it fair that even though the cops down there might know who did it nothing will probably ever happen to those men? It ain't. But you just gotta understand that's the way it is and keep on steppin'."

10. "I think we've got our fingers in God's beard and as we drive along we're tickling him."

Short Answer Unit Test 2 *The Watsons Go to Birmingham –1963*

IV. Essay

Describe the growth of Kenny and of Byron as characters throughout the novel. Use examples from the novel in your response.

Short Answer Unit Test 2 *The Watsons Go to Birmingham –1963*

V. Vocabulary Part 1
　　Listen to the vocabulary word and spell it. After you have spelled all the words, go back and write down the definitions.

　　WORD　　　　　　　　　　　　　　　DEFINITION

1. _____　　_____

2. _____　　_____

3. _____　　_____

4. _____　　_____

5. _____　　_____

6. _____　　_____

7. _____　　_____

8. _____　　_____

9. _____　　_____

10. _____　　_____

Vocabulary Part 2: Place the letter of the matching definition on the blank line.

_____ 1. bound　　　　　　A. clenching; grinding
_____ 2. dazzle　　　　　　B. very low-paid worker
_____ 3. executed　　　　　C. one who does something disloyal
_____ 4. gnashing　　　　　D. certain to do something
_____ 5. intimidate　　　　E. very important
_____ 6. peon　　　　　　　F. put to death
_____ 7. sanitation　　　　G. a large number
_____ 8. slew　　　　　　　H. related to health and cleanliness
_____ 9. traitor　　　　　　I. amaze
_____ 10. vital　　　　　　 J. create a feeling of fear in someone

ANSWER KEY SHORT ANSWER UNIT TEST 2
The Watsons Go to Birmingham –1963

I. Matching/Identification
Directions: Place the letter of the matching definition on the blank line.

C   1. squirrel   A. Dad did not keep his with the rest of the family

H   2. dove   B. "pinnacle of Western Civilization"

A   3. toothbrush   C. Rufus and Cody ate this animal in stew back home

G   4. bathroom   D. record player: True-Tone AB-700

J   5. mirror   E. family car: 1948 Plymouth

B   6. pine tree   F. "World Famous Watson Pet ____"

D   7. Ultra Glide   G. there was one for "Coloreds Only" in Birmingham

E   8. "Brown Bomber"   H. Byron killed and buried this animal

F   9. hospital   I. site of bombings

I   10. church   J. place on car where Byron's lips froze

II. Short Answer

1. What did Momma catch Byron doing in the bathroom and what did she say she would do to him? Was Momma successful in carrying out her threat? Explain why or why not.
    Byron got caught lighting matches in the bathroom. Momma said she would burn his fingers. No, she was not successful. She tried to burn Byron's fingers but Joey kept blowing out the matches.

2. What news did the parents tell the children while they were all sitting in the car listening to the records? What were their reasons for this news?
    The parents told the children that the family would soon be driving to Alabama. Byron would be spending the summer or maybe the next school year with Grandma Sands. They said that Byron was driving them crazy and they would not have the nonsense going on any more.

Answer Key Short Answer Unit Test 2 *The Watsons Go to Birmingham –1963*

3. How did Kenny think of Rufus and why?
    Kenny thought of Rufus as his personal savior because when he first met Rufus he realized that the other kids would begin teasing Rufus instead of him.

4. What fictional characters did Kenny use to describe how he expected the meeting between Grandma Sands and Byron to go? What characters did he use to describe how the meeting actually went? How did Kenny feel about the reality of the meeting?
    Kenny thought the meeting would be like King Kong meeting Godzilla. Instead it was like King Kong meets Bambi. Kenny thought it was like all the fight was out of Byron.

5. Describe the conversation between Joey and Kenny back at Grandma Sands's house after Kenny came back from the church. What did Joey tell Kenny about her time in the church that morning?
    Joey asked Kenny how he got back home so fast and why he changed his clothes. Kenny thought that the Wool Pooh was taking Joey around to say good-bye. Kenny thanked Joey for saving his life. Joey asked him if he was crazy. Then Joey asked him whose shoe he had with him, since she was carrying both of hers. She told Kenny it was hot so she went outside. She saw Kenny and chased him down the street.

6. Which one of the children were the parents the most worried about after the family came back from Birmingham? Why?
    They were most worried about Kenny. He had been disappearing and they did not know where he was going. They wondered if Mr. Robert's friend had been right when he told them he had seen Kenny in the church after the bombing.

7. Summarize what happened when Bryon took Kenny into the bathroom. What did Byron say Kenny should think about? How did Kenny feel at the end of the story?
    Byron took Kenny into the bathroom to show him a hair on his (Byron's) chin. When Kenny looked in the mirror and saw himself looking so sad he started crying. He asked Byron why the men would want to hurt kids by bombing the church. Kenny said he was ashamed because he left Joey in the church when he thought the Wool Pooh had her. Byron said Kenny should think about why Joey was not in the church. He said it was a part of Kenny that took Joey out of the church. At the end of the story Kenny felt better and was laughing.

8. What did Kenny think about making Byron spend a whole summer in the heat? How did Byron seem to be taking it?
    Kenny thought that spending the whole summer in the heat was more than even Byron deserved. Byron seemed like he was enjoying himself.

Answer Key Short Answer Unit Test 2 *The Watsons Go to Birmingham –1963*

9. What was the title of Momma's notebook? What was on the cover? What were the contents?

   Momma called her notebook, "The Watsons Go to Birmingham–1963. She drew a bee and a flower on the cover. Inside, she had written down plans for the trip; where, when, and what they would eat, how much money they would spend, when they would take rest and bathroom stops, who got the windows each day, and who would clean up the car.

10. Why was Rufus upset with Kenny? What happened as a result? How did Kenny feel? How was the problem solved?

    Larry Dunn made fun of Rufus and Cody because of their pants. When the other kids laughed, Kenny laughed along with them. Rufus stopped sitting next to Kenny and playing at his house. Kenny felt sad and told his mother what had happened. His mother visited Rufus's house and the next day Rufus and Cody came over to Kenny's house. Kenny apologized and the boys became friends again.

III. Quotations
Directions: Identify the speaker and discuss the significance of the following quotations.

1. "Oh, Mom-ma! Hel' me! Geh me offa 'ere!"

   Byron said this. When he and Kenny were scraping the ice off the car windows, Byron kissed his image in the side mirror and his lips froze to the mirror. Momma pulled Byron's lips off of the mirror.

2. "Don't you pay no mind to them little fools, they ain't happy lest they draggin' someone down." Y'all just sit next to Poindexter, he don't bother no one."

   The bus driver said this to Rufus and Cody their first day on the bus. The other kids had started teasing them. The bus driver stopped the other kids and told the boys to sit with Kenny.

3. "I can't believe it. You really gonna start serving welfare food in this house? You really gonna make me go embarrass myself by signing a welfare list for some groceries like a blanged peon?"

   Byron said this to Momma. Momma told the boys to go to the store and told Byron to sign for the groceries. He thought that meant they were on welfare. He was embarrassed to sign a welfare list like a peon. He made Kenny sign for the food. Byron's assumption was not correct. The family was not on welfare. Mr. Watson had arranged to pay the bill all at once.

4. "Well, that's what being a grown-up is like. At first it's scary but then before you realize, with a lot of practice, you have it under control. Hopefully you'll have lots of time to practice being grown-up before you actually have to do it."

Answer Key Short Answer Unit Test 2 *The Watsons Go to Birmingham –1963*
III. Quotations, continued

Dad said this to Kenny. Kenny was wondering how parents knew what to do. He had told Dad that he would never understand what to do as a grown up. He said he would never be as good a parent as his parents were.

5. " 'Cuz, boy, this he-uh is the deep South you-all is gonna be drivin' thoo. Y'all colored folks cain't be jes' pullin' up tuh any ol' way-uh an be 'spectin' tuh get no room uh no food, yuh heah, boy? I said yuh heah what I'm sayin', boy?"
Dad did this hillbilly imitation on the trip. Kenny had asked why they didn't just drive until Dad got tired and then stop. This was Dad's reply.

6. "What you expect? You seen her. That bird's as old as dirt. She's so old I bet she used to step over dinosaur turds. I ain't gonna have her death on my hands."
Byron said this to Kenny. Kenny had expressed disappointment that Byron was not acting up while they were in Birmingham. Kenny thought all the fight was out of Byron.

7. "If Kenny wants to take his stupid little behind down there and get snatched, let him."
Byron said this. He and Kenny and Joey were in Birmingham. They were looking at a No Trespassing sign for Collier's Landing. Kenny wanted to go there anyway but Byron did not.

8. "Shut up and cry if you want to."
Byron said this to Kenny. It happened after their return from Birmingham. Byron took Kenny into the bathroom to show him a hair on his (Byron's) chin. When Kenny looked in the mirror and saw himself looking so sad he started crying. He asked Byron why the men would want to hurt kids by bombing the church. Kenny said he was ashamed because he left Joey in the church when he thought the Wool Pooh had her

9. "Kenny, things ain't ever going to be fair. How's it fair that two grown men could hate Negroes so much that they'd kill some kids just to stop them from going to school? How's it fair that even though the cops down there might know who did it nothing will probably ever happen to those men? It ain't. But you just gotta understand that that's the way it is and keep on steppin'."
Byron said this to Kenny. They were still in the bathroom and Kenny had asked Byron why the men had bombed the church. He said it wasn't fair.

10. "I think we've got our fingers in God's beard and as we drive along we're tickling him."
Dad said this on the trip to Birmingham. He was describing their drive through the Appalachian Mountains.

Answer Key Short Answer Unit Test 2 *The Watsons Go to Birmingham –1963*

IV. Essay

Describe the growth of Kenny and of Byron as characters throughout the novel. Use examples from the novel in your response.

(for teacher notes)

V. Vocabulary Part 1

	WORD	DEFINITION
1.	_____	_____
2.	_____	_____
3.	_____	_____
4.	_____	_____
5.	_____	_____
6.	_____	_____
7.	_____	_____
8.	_____	_____
9.	_____	_____
10.	_____	_____

Vocabulary Part 2: Place the letter of the matching definition on the blank line.

D	1. bound	A. clenching; grinding
I	2. dazzle	B. very low-paid worker
F	3. executed	C. one who does something disloyal
A	4. gnashing	D. certain to do something
J	5. intimidate	E. very important
B	6. peon	F. put to death
H	7. sanitation	G. a large number
G	8. slew	H. related to health and cleanliness
C	9. traitor	I. amaze
E	10. vital	J. create a feeling of fear in someone

ADVANCED SHORT ANSWER UNIT TEST *The Watsons Go to Birmingham –1963*

I. Matching/Identification
Directions: Place the letter of the matching definition on the blank line.

_____ 1. squirrel   A. Dad did not keep his with the rest of the family

_____ 2. dove   B. pinnacle of Western Civilization"

_____ 3. toothbrush   C. Rufus and Cody ate this animal in stew back home

_____ 4. bathroom   D. record player: True-Tone AB-700 ___

_____ 5. mirror   E. family car: 1948 Plymouth _____

_____ 6. pine tree   F. "World Famous Watson Pet ____"

_____ 7. Ultra Glide   G. there was one for "Coloreds Only" in Birmingham

_____ 8. "Brown Bomber"   H. Byron killed and buried this animal

_____ 9. hospital   I. place on car where Byron's lips froze

II. Short Answer
Directions: Write a detailed answer for each question.

1. Describe what Kenny did and saw when he got to the church. Describe the conversation between Joey and Kenny back at Grandma Sands's house after Kenny came back from the church. What did Joey tell Kenny about her time in the church that morning?

2. Summarize what happened when Bryon took Kenny into the bathroom after they had been back from Birmingham for a while.

Advanced Short Answer Unit Test *The Watsons Go to Birmingham –1963*

3. Describe the mood of the story. Explain when the mood changes, how it changes, and why. Include how you felt about the mood change and explain why.

4. Describe the growth of Kenny and of Byron as characters throughout the novel. Use examples from the novel in your response.

5. The author incorporated a real event, the church bombing, into a fictional story. How effective was this device? Did it add to or take away from your enjoyment of the story?

Advanced Short Answer Unit Test *The Watsons Go to Birmingham –1963*

III. Quotations
Directions: Identify the speaker and discuss the significance of each of the following quotations.

1. "Oh, Mom-ma! Hel' me! Geh me offa 'ere!"

2. "Don't you pay no mind to them little fools, they ain't happy lest they draggin' someone down." Y'all just sit next to Poindexter, he don't bother no one."

3. "I thought you was my friend. I didn't think you was like all them other people." I thought you was different."

4. "Get the hell out of here, what you starin' at? Them apples got me sick, you little cross-eyed punk! Get out of here."

5. "But Mommy, it's white."

Advanced Short Answer Unit Test *The Watsons Go to Birmingham –1963*

III. Quotations, continued

6. "I think we've got our fingers in God's beard and as we drive along we're tickling him."

7. "What you expect? You seen her. That bird's as old as dirt. She's so old I bet she used to step over dinosaur turds. I ain't gonna have her death on my hands."

8. "Where'd you go? How'd you get back here so fast? How come you changed your clothes?"

9. "Shut up and cry if you want to."

10. "You think I don't know you waiting for some stupid magic powers or genies or a angel to make you feel better?"

Advanced Short Answer Unit Test *The Watsons Go to Birmingham –1963*

IV. Vocabulary

Directions: Listen to the words and write them down. After you have written down all of the words, write a paragraph in which you use all the words. The paragraph must in some way relate to the book *The Watsons Go to Birmingham –1963*.

MULTIPLE CHOICE UNIT TEST 1 *The Watsons Go to Birmingham –1963*

I. Matching/Identification:
Directions: Place the letter of the matching definition on the blank line.

_____ 1. Kenny   A. little sister; left the bombed church

_____ 2. Joey   B. where grandmother lived

_____ 3. Byron   C. forced to play "Great Carp Escape"

_____ 4. Larry Dunn   D. helped Byron with his conk hairstyle

_____ 5. Rufus   E. narrator of story

_____ 6. Buphead   F. where family lived

_____ 7. LJ Jones   G. Rufus's brother; shot squirrels

_____ 8. Birmingham   H. stole narrator's toy dinosaurs

_____ 9. Flint   I. older brother; helped narrator at end of story

_____ 10. Cody   J. personal savior to story's narrator

II. Multiple Choice

1. Dad talked with Kenny about the reasons they were sending Byron to Alabama. What did Dad tell Kenny?
    A. Grandma Sands had raised ten boys and they were all fine men. The parents thought she could get Byron to straighten up.
    B. Byron was taking up too much of their time and attention. They were sending him away so they could concentrate on raising the other two children.
    C. They thought that spending some time in the South would open Byron's eyes to the way the world could be.
    D. They felt like failures as parents and needed help.

2. Did Grandma Sands look the way Kenny expected her to look?
    A. Yes, she did.
    B. No, she did not.

Multiple Choice Unit Test 1 *The Watsons Go to Birmingham –1963*

II. Multiple Choice, continued

3. Who played "The Great Carp Escape," and how did they play?
    A. Larry threw things that belonged to the other boys in the lake and other boys ran in to get them. When they tried to get out of the lake, Larry hit them with rocks.
    B. LJ stole things from the other boys. To get them back, the boys had to pay and also do several jobs for LJ.
    C. Byron and Buphead threw someone who had bothered Kenny against the chain link fence over and over. The boy was supposed to try and get away.
    D. Boys from the high school put boys from the elementary school in fishing nets and hung them in trees. The boys had to get themselves out of the nets.

4. What did Byron do when Kenny was out of the whirlpool?
    A. Bryon beat up Kenny for being reckless.
    B. Bryon ran home to get towels and a blanket.
    C. Byron kissed the top of Kenny's head.
    D. Bryon gave Kenny CPR to help him breathe again.

5. Why was Rufus upset with Kenny?
    A. Kenny would not share his lunch dessert with Cody and Rufus.
    B. Kenny invited Rufus to play but would not invite Cody. Since Rufus had to watch over Cody, then Rufus could not go to Kenny's house.
    C. Larry Dunn made fun of Rufus and Cody because of their pants. When the other kids laughed, Kenny laughed along with them.
    D. The teacher told Rufus to help Kenny with some math. Kenny got insulted and refused to let Rufus help.

6. True or False: After Rufus began sitting next to Kenny in class, both boys got picked on.
    A. True
    B. False

7. What did Momma tell Byron to do when he went to Mr. Mitchell's store?
    A. She told him to use money from his piggy bank to pay.
    B. She told him to offer to work for Mr. Mitchell in payment for the food.
    C. She told him to ask if he could pay the next week.
    D. She told him to sign for the groceries.

Multiple Choice Unit Test 1 *The Watsons Go to Birmingham –1963*

8. What did his parents do about Bryon's new hairdo?
   A. Dad shaved Byron's head bald.
   B. Momma took him to her hairdresser to get it fixed.
   C. They said he would have to live with it.
   D. They made Byron wear a dress until the hair was back to normal.

9. What happened to Byron when he and Kenny were scraping the ice off the car windows?
   A. Byron kissed his image in the side mirror and his lips froze to the mirror.
   B. Kenny rubbed the side window glass so hard that he put his hand through it.
   C. Byron pushed the back of the car and it rolled down the street.
   D. Kenny worked faster than Byron and Byron got angry.

10. What did Kenny tell Byron when they were in the bathroom?
    A. Kenny said he was ashamed because he left Joey in the church.
    B. Kenny said he had nightmares about the blood and the smoke.
    C. Kenny said he thought he would never get better.
    D. Kenny said that if Byron had not misbehaved they would not have been in Birmingham.

Multiple Choice Unit Test 1 *The Watsons Go to Birmingham –1963*
III. Quotations Directions: Match the two parts of each quotation.

1. "Naw, man, keep your head straight and look at me sideways." I did it. "See?

2. "Oh, yeah. They're a laugh a minute down there.

3. "I want you to carefully note how advanced this second-grade student is, and I particularly want you to be aware of the effect his skills have upon you.

4. "I thought you was my friend. I didn't think you was like all them other people.

5. "You grew up to be a fine-lookin' boy.

6. "You think I don't know you waiting for some stupid magic powers___

7. He's been disappearing___

8. "Get the hell out of here, what you starin' at?

9. If you ever, ever . . . play with–no, if you ever even look at . . . another match in this house I will personally, by myself I will burn . . .

10. "Don't you pay no mind to them little fools, they ain't happy lest they draggin' someone down.

A. I thought you was different."

B. Them apples got me sick, you little cross-eyed punk! Get out of here."

C. or genies or a angel to make you feel better?"

D. Let's see, where was that 'Coloreds Only' bathroom downtown?"

E. You was so puny when you was born you nearly worried us crazy. Got strong, too."

F. I want you to be aware that some of our kids read at miraculous levels."

G. Hours go by and I don't know where he is."

H. You ain't cockeyed no more, your eyes is straight as a arrow now!"

I. not just one finger, I will burn your entire hand, then send you to juvenile home!"

J. Y'all just sit next to Poindexter, he don't bother no one."

Multiple Choice Unit Test 1 *The Watsons Go to Birmingham –1963*
IV. Vocabulary Part 1
Directions: Place the letter of the matching definition on the blank line.

_____ 1. automatically   A. having greater age or higher rank
_____ 2. dispositioned   B. stop; restrict
_____ 3. emulate   C. not able to feel emotions
_____ 4. hostile   D. put up with
_____ 5. numb   E. more clever at deceiving
_____ 6. seniority   F. aid in the form of money and other benefits
_____ 7. stunt   G. done without thought
_____ 8. tolerate   H. full of hatred or anger
_____ 9. welfare   I. related to mood or temperament
_____ 10. wilier   J. try to be like someone else

IV. Vocabulary Part 2
Directions: Mark the letter next to the word that matches the definition.

11. certain to do something
    A. bound
    B. hostile
    C. pathetic
    D. sobby

12. in a posture low to the ground
    A. wailing
    B. slew
    C. crouched
    D. gnashing

13. produce or make
    A. infect
    B. generate
    C. jabbering
    D. nibble

14. unplanned
    A. haphazardly
    B. automatically
    C. ultimate
    D. staggered

15. put into a sleeplike condition
    A. tresspassing
    B. hypnotized
    C. rabies
    D. scowl

16. a spiral current of water
    A. sonic boom
    B. curveball
    C. whirlpool
    D. peon

17. a breed of large fish, including goldfish
    A. dazzle
    B. conk
    C. mug
    D. carp

18. very important
    A. vital
    B. wilier
    C. emulate
    D. numb

19. listening in when the speaker does not know it
    A. mumbling
    B. determined
    C. incapable
    D. eavesdropping

20. not generous
    A. jive
    B. stingy
    C. peon
    D. hostile

MULTIPLE CHOICE UNIT TEST 2 *The Watsons Go to Birmingham –1963*

I. Matching/Identification
Directions: Place the letter of the matching definition on the blank line.

_____ 1. squirrel   A. Dad did not keep his with the rest of the family

_____ 2. dove   B. pinnacle of Western Civilization"

_____ 3. toothbrush   C. Rufus and Cody ate this animal in stew back home

_____ 4. bathroom   D. record player: True-Tone AB-700 ___

_____ 5. mirror   E. family car: 1948 Plymouth _____

_____ 6. pine tree   F. "World Famous Watson Pet ____"

_____ 7. Ultra Glide   G. there was one for "Coloreds Only" in Birmingham

_____ 8. "Brown Bomber"   H. Byron killed and buried this animal

_____ 9. hospital   I. site of bombings

_____ 10. church   J. place on car where Byron's lips froze

II. Short Answer

1. What did Momma catch Byron doing?
    A. Byron got caught smoking cigarettes in back of the house.
    B. Byron got caught lighting matches in the bathroom.
    C. Byron got caught stealing money from his mother's purse.
    D. Byron got caught forging Dad's signature on his report card.

2. While they were all sitting in the car, the parents told the children the family____.
    A. would soon be driving to Alabama. Byron would be spending the summer or maybe the next school with Grandma Sands.
    B. would soon be driving to New York. Byron would be attending military school there. Grandma Sands was paying for it.
    C. would soon be moving to Alabama. The family was going to move in with Grandma Sands.
    D. would soon be moving to Montana. They bought a ranch so the children would not be exposed to city life any more. Grandma Sands would move in with them.

Multiple Choice Unit Test 2 *The Watsons Go to Birmingham –1963*

II. Short Answer, continued

3. How did Kenny think of Rufus?
    A. Kenny thought of Rufus as a country hick.
    B. Kenny thought of Rufus as his personal savior.
    C. Kenny thought of Rufus as a kind and gentle person.
    D. Kenny thought of Rufus as a wild rebel.

4. What fictional characters did Kenny use to describe how he expected the meeting between Grandma Sands and Byron to go? What characters did he use to describe how the meeting actually went?
    A. Kenny thought the meeting would be like Popeye meeting Brutus. Instead it was like Popeye meets Olive Oyl.
    B. Kenny thought the meeting would be like Tarzan meeting the lion. Instead it was like Tarzan meets Jane.
    C. Kenny thought the meeting would be like Superman meeting Lex Luthor. Instead it was like Superman meets Ma Kent.
    D. Kenny thought the meeting would be like King Kong meeting Godzilla. Instead it was like King Kong meets Bambi.

5. What did Joey tell Kenny about her time in the church the morning of the bombing?
    A. She said she ran when she heard the noise.
    B. She said she had gone to the park instead of church.
    C. She said saw Kenny and chased him down the street.
    D. She said she came home early because she was tired.

6. Who were the parents the most worried about after the bombing?
    A. Joey
    B. Grandma Sands
    C. Byron
    D. Kenny

7. What did Kenny tell Byron when they were in the bathroom?
    A. Kenny said he was ashamed because he left Joey in the church.
    B. Kenny said he had nightmares about the blood and the smoke.
    C. Kenny said he thought he would never get better.
    D. Kenny said that if Byron had not misbehaved they would not have been in Birmingham.

Multiple Choice Unit Test 2 *The Watsons Go to Birmingham –1963*

8. What did Kenny think about making Byron spend a whole summer in the heat?
    A. Kenny thought that the punishment was just right for Byron.
    B. Kenny thought that Byron deserved a whole year of the heat.
    C. Kenny thought that Byron had already been punished enough.
    D. Kenny thought it was more than even Byron deserved.

9. Which statement does not describe something about Momma's notebook?
    A. The title of the notebook was "The Weird Watsons on the Road."
    B. She had drawn a bee and a flower on the cover.
    C. Inside, she had written down plans for the trip, including expenses.
    D. She had a list of who got the windows each day.

10. Why was Rufus upset with Kenny?
    A. Kenny would not share his lunch dessert with Cody and Rufus.
    B. Kenny invited Rufus to play but would not invite Cody. Since Rufus had to watch over Cody, then Rufus could not go to Kenny's house.
    C. Larry Dunn made fun of Rufus and Cody because of their pants. When the other kids laughed, Kenny laughed along with them.
    D. The teacher told Rufus to help Kenny with some math. Kenny got insulted and refused to let Rufus help.

Multiple Choice Unit Test 2 *The Watsons Go to Birmingham –1963*

III. Quotations Directions: Match the two parts of each quotation.

1. "Oh, Mom-ma! Hel' me!

2. "Don't you pay no mind to them little fools, they ain't happy lest they draggin' someone down.

3. "I can't believe it.

4. "Well, that's what being a grown-up is like. At first it's scary but then . . . .

5. "Y'all colored folks cain't be jes' pullin' up tuh any ol' way-uh an be 'spectin' . . .

6. "What you expect? You seen her. That bird's as old as dirt.

7. "If Kenny wants to take his stupid little behind down there and get snatched, . . .

8. . "Shut up and . . .

9. "Kenny, things ain't ever going to be fair. . . . It ain't. . . .

10. "I think we've got our fingers in God's beard

A. tuh get no room uh no food, yuh heah, boy? I said yuh heah what I'm sayin', boy?"

B. let him."

C. You really gonna start serving welfare food in this house?"

D. and as we drive along we're tickling him."

E. Y'all just sit next to Poindexter, he don't bother no one."

F. cry if you want to."

G. I ain't gonna have her death on my hands."

H. Geh me offa 'ere!"

I. But you just gotta understand that that's the way it is and keep on steppin'."

J. before you realize, with a lot of practice, you have it under control."

Multiple Choice Unit Test 2 *The Watsons Go to Birmingham –1963*
Vocabulary Part 1:
Directions: Place the letter of the matching definition on the blank line.

         1. bound   A. clenching; grinding
         2. dazzle   B. very low-paid worker
         3. executed   C. one who does something disloyal
         4. gnashing   D. certain to do something
         5. intimidate   E. very important
         6. peon   F. put to death
         7. sanitation   G. a large number
         8. slew   H. related to health and cleanliness
         9. traitor   I. amaze
        10. vital   J. create a feeling of fear in someone

IV. Vocabulary Part 2
Directions: Mark the letter next to the word that matches the definition.

11. a style that straightens curly hair
    A. scowl
    B. conk
    C. snitch
    D. mugs

12. highest quality
    A. hostile
    B. punctual
    C. ultimate
    D. snitch

13. distractions
    A. thugs
    B. tolerate
    C. curveballs
    D. dispositions

14. very funny
    A. wilier
    B. vital
    C. hilarious
    D. pathetic

15. talking very quickly
    A. jabbering
    B. trespassing
    C. eavesdropping
    D. wailing

16. damage to limbs caused by freezing
    A. jive
    B. rabies
    C. sonic boom
    D. frostbite

17. speed
    A. stunt
    B. pace
    C. peon
    D. slew

18. try to be like someone else
    A. generate
    B. emulate
    C. infect
    D. square

19. on time
    A. haphazardly
    B. mature
    C. seniority
    D. punctual

20. not able to do something
    A. staggered
    B. traitor
    C. tolerate
    D. incapable

ANSWER SHEET MULTIPLE CHOICE UNIT TEST 1
The Watsons Go to Birmingham - 1963

I. Matching	III. Quotations	IV. Vocabulary
1.	1.	1.
2.	2.	2.
3.	3.	3.
4.	4.	4.
5.	5.	5.
6.	6.	6.
7.	7.	7.
8.	8.	8.
9.	9.	9.
10.	10.	10.
		11.
		12.

II. Multiple Choice

1. (A) (B) (C) (D)
2. (A) (B) (C) (D)
3. (A) (B) (C) (D)
4. (A) (B) (C) (D)
5. (A) (B) (C) (D)
6. (A) (B) (C) (D)
7. (A) (B) (C) (D)
8. (A) (B) (C) (D)
9. (A) (B) (C) (D)
10. (A) (B) (C) (D)

IV. Vocabulary (continued):
13.
14.
15.
16.
17.
18.
19.
20.

ANSWER SHEET KEY MULTIPLE CHOICE UNIT TEST 1
The Watsons Go to Birmingham -1963

I. Matching	III. Quotations	IV. Vocabulary
1. E	1. H	1. G
2. A	2. D	2. I
3. I	3. F	3. J
4. C	4. A	4. H
5. J	5. E	5. C
6. D	6. C	6. A
7. H	7. G	7. B
8. B	8. B	8. D
9. F	9. I	9. F
10. G	10. J	10. E
		11. A

II. Multiple Choice

1. (A) (B) ( ) (D)
2. (A) ( ) (C) (D)
3. (A) (B) ( ) (D)
4. (A) (B) ( ) (D)
5. (A) (B) ( ) (D)
6. (A) ( ) (C) (D)
7. (A) (B) (C) ( )
8. ( ) (B) (C) (D)
9. ( ) (B) (C) (D)
10. ( ) (B) (C) (D)

12. C
13. B
14. A
15. B
16. C
17. D
18. A
19. D
20. B

ANSWER SHEET KEY MULTIPLE CHOICE UNIT TEST 2
The Watsons Go to Birmingham -1963

I. Matching	III. Quotations	IV. Vocabulary
1. C	1. H	1. D
2. H	2. E	2. I
3. A	3. C	3. F
4. G	4. J	4. A
5. J	5. A	5. J
6. B	6. G	6. B
7. D	7. B	7. H
8. E	8. F	8. G
9. F	9. I	9. C
10. I	10. D	10. E
		11. B
		12. C
		13. C
		14. C
		15. A
		16. D
		17. B
		18. B
		19. D
		20. D

II. Multiple Choice
1. (A) ( ) (C) (D)
2. ( ) (B) (C) (D)
3. (A) ( ) (C) (D)
4. (A) (B) (C) ( )
5. (A) (B) ( ) (D)
6. (A) (B) (C) ( )
7. ( ) (B) (C) (D)
8. (A) (B) (C) ( )
9. ( ) (B) (C) (D)
10. (A) (B) ( ) (D)

UNIT RESOURCES

BULLETIN BOARD IDEAS *The Watsons Go to Birmingham –1963*

1. Save one corner of the board for the best of students' *The Watsons Go to Birmingham – 1963* writing assignments. You may want to use background maps of Michigan and Alabama and the states in between to represent the setting of the novel.

2. Take one of the word search puzzles from the extra activities packet and with a marker copy it over in a large size on the bulletin board. Write the clue words to find to one side. Invite students prior to and after class to find the words and circle them on the bulletin board.

3. Have students find or draw pictures that they think resemble the people and scenery in the book.

4. Invite students to help make an interactive bulletin board quiz. Give each student a half-sheet of paper (about 4"x5') folded in half so that it can open. On the outside flap, have each student write a description of one of the characters in the text. On the inside, they will write the name of the character. You can staple or tack these papers to the bulletin board so that the students can read the descriptions and lift the flaps to find the answers.

5. Collect and display pictures of Alabama, Michigan, other parts of the United States around 1963. Try to include some pictures that show evidence of racial discrimination, automobiles styles, hair dos, etc.

6. Display articles about the bombing of the church in Birmingham and other Civil Rights era related bombings, marches, etc.

7. Display articles about Christopher Paul Curtis.

8. Have students design postcards depicting the settings of the book.

EXTRA ACTIVITIES PACKET *The Watsons Go to Birmingham –1963*

One of the difficulties in teaching a novel is that all students don't read at the same speed. One student who likes to read may take the book home and finish it in a day or two. Sometimes a few students finish the in-class assignments early. The problem, then, is finding suitable extra activities for students.

One thing that helps is to keep a little library in the classroom. For this unit on *The Watsons Go to Birmingham –1963* you might check out from the school or public library other books about the Civil Rights movement, segregation around 1963, and other books set in that time frame.

Your students who have reading difficulties, or speak English as a second language may benefit from listening to all or part of the book on tape. *The Watsons Go to Birmingham –1963* is available commercially, or you may want to have an adult or a student who reads well tape record the book for you.

Other things you may keep on hand are word search puzzles. Several puzzles relating directly to *The Watsons Go to Birmingham –1963* are included in the unit. Feel free to duplicate them.

Some students may like to draw. You might devise a contest or allow some extra-credit grade for students who draw characters or scenes from *The Watsons Go to Birmingham –1963*. Note, too, that if the students do not want to keep their drawings you may pick up some extra bulletin board materials this way. If you have a contest and you supply the prize. You could, possibly, make the drawing itself a nonrefundable entry fee.

Have maps, a globe, and travel brochures on hand for easy reference. Travel agencies and automobile clubs are good sources for these materials.

The pages which follow contain games, puzzles, and worksheets. The keys, when appropriate, immediately follow the puzzle or worksheet. There are two main groups of activities: one group for the unit; that is, generally relating to the *The Watsons Go to Birmingham –1963* text, and another group of activities related strictly to the *The Watsons Go to Birmingham –1963* vocabulary.

Directions for the games, puzzles, and worksheets are self-explanatory. The object here is to provide you with extra materials you may use in any way you choose.

MORE ACTIVITIES *The Watsons Go to Birmingham –1963*

1. Pick one of the incidents for students to dramatize. Encourage students to write dialog for the characters. (Perhaps you could assign various stories to different groups of students so more than one story could be acted and more students could participate.)

2. Have students design a bulletin board (ready to be put up; not just sketched) for *The Watsons Go to Birmingham –1963*.

3. Invite someone to talk to the class about the Civil Rights era and/or discrimination.

4. Have someone from a military base or police department come and talk about their training in preparation for bombings and other acts of violence.

5. Ask someone from a social services agency to talk to the class about their efforts with juvenile delinquents and their families.

6. Help students design and produce a talk show. Choose one of the story incidents as the topic. The host will interview the various characters. (Students should make up the questions they want the host to ask the characters.)

7. Have students work in pairs to create an interview with one of the characters. One student should be the interviewer and the other should be the interviewee. Students can work together to compose questions for the interviewer to ask. Each pair of students could present their interview to the class.

8. Invite students who have read other books by Christopher Paul Curtis to present booktalks to the class.

9. Invite students who have read other books on a similar topic as *The Watsons Go to Birmingham –1963* to present booktalks to the class.

10. Use some of the related topics (noted earlier for an in-class library) as topics for research, reports, or written papers, or as topics for guest speakers.

11. Invite someone who has lived in one of the areas mentioned in the book to speak to the class.

12. Have students hold small group discussions related to topics in the book. Assign a recorder and a speaker for each group. Have the speaker from each group make a report to the class.

MORE ACTIVITIES *The Watsons Go to Birmingham –1963*

13. Use the Internet to take a virtual field trip to the site of the Birmingham church bombings and also read the newspaper articles about the bombings. Enter the keywords "Birmingham church bombings" for several references. NOTE: Teachers should carefully preview these sites as there are several photographs that graphically show the effects of the bombings and other violence.

14. Research life of African Americans in the United States between 1865 and 1969.

15. Research one of the individuals or organizations that was working to end racial discrimination mentioned in the Epilogue, such as the Rev. Dr. Martin Luther King, Jr., Medgar Evans, the NAACP, SLCL, or CORE. Prepare a report for the class using a computer and presentation software.

16. If possible, speak with someone whose relatives or friends were present during the bombings or were otherwise affected by or involved in the fights for Civil Rights during the 1960s. Report on their experiences. (Note: Caution students to be sensitive if they do this activity.)

17. Bring in music from the 1960s such as the songs mentioned in the book and play it for the class.

18. Write additional chapters for the book, telling what was happening in other parts of the United States during 1963.

19. Find out how African Americans live in the United States today.

20. Find out more about the history of the Sixteenth Avenue Baptist Church in Birmingham where the bombings took place.

WORD SEARCH - Watsons Go To Birmingham –1963

Words are placed backwards, forward, diagonally, up and down. Words listed below are included in the maze. Circle the hidden vocabulary words in the maze.

```
A M A B A L A D S J F O U R B H K R T N
T A Z T G G X W H M U M T R T H X O W N
W G K Z D O C R O Y S V O E Y X B B I B
K I N G X D R A E B S W E L F A R E N V
F C N J J U I O W C N T G N L X K R X C
L W Z D F J J N A E O S N D I V O T D F
D H Q U O Y T R O W I R U B Y L V A B C
T I S S T W Y Y D S C R D M S R E Y A L
Z R C K K A S N A I A P D M M H N R M M
Z L H E C N L V H Z L U Q V P E T R B J
C P P Z B P I K S A D G R U M N R A I S
N O T E B O O K I N K O B S I B L L S G
G O U G R H X D D N H D V L T O P Z A W
V L C C C K A R E O G Z F E C M M Y N M
J C N T H R E K W R G I L C H B C Y D K
P O O H T N G M S Y F L J A E S Z O S N
K D Y L I G M Z K B F L L R L A G C N Q
B Y U P D R O W N E D A W P L F L Y N K
```

ALABAMA	COUCH	JUVENILE	PINE	TALKING
BALD	DINOSAURS	KING	POOH	TEETH
BAMBI	DOVE	LARRY	RECORD	TWIN
BEARD	DROWNED	LAYERS	ROBERT	ULTRA
BOMB	FLINT	LAZY	RUFUS	WEIRD
BROWN	FLY	LJ	SANDS	WELFARE
BUPHEAD	FOUR	MAGIC	SAVIOR	WHIRLPOOL
BYRON	GOD	MITCHELL	SCARY	WINDOWS
CARP	GODZILLA	NAZIS	SHOE	YAK
CODY	ICEBOX	NOTEBOOK	SUMMER	
CONK	JOEY	OVEN	SWEDISH	

WORD SEARCH ANSWER KEY - Watsons Go To Birmingham –1963

Words are placed backwards, forward, diagonally, up and down. Words listed below are included in the maze. Circle the hidden vocabulary words in the maze.

```
A  M  A  B  A  L  A        S  J  F  O  U  R  B  H     R        T
   A              G            H     U     R  T           O        W
W  G              O     R  O  Y  V  O  E  Y     B  B     I
K  I  N  G        D  R  A  E  B  S  W  E  L  F  A  R  E  N
      C  N           U  I  O  W  C     N  L        K  R
      W        D  F     J  N  A  E  O  S     D        O  T  D
      H        U  O        R  O     I  R  U        L     V  A  B
      I  S        T  W  Y        S     R  D  M  S  R  E  Y  A  L
      R  C           A  S     A  I  A     D     M  H  N  R  M
         L  E           L  V  H  Z     U        P  E  T  R  B
C  P           B     I  K  S  A  D  G  R  U  M  N     R  A  I
N  O  T  E  B  O  O  K     I  N     O  B  S  I  B        L  S
   O  U           R     X     D  N     D  V  L  T  O           A
      L     C              A     E  O  G  Z  F  E  C  M        N
      C        H  R  E        W  R     I  L  C  H  B  C  Y     D
P  O  O  H  T     N           S  Y        L  J  A  E     Z  O  S
   D     L  I                 B           L     R  L  A           N
   Y  U  P  D  R  O  W  N  E  D  A        P  L  F  L  Y           K
```

ALABAMA	COUCH	JUVENILE	PINE	TALKING
BALD	DINOSAURS	KING	POOH	TEETH
BAMBI	DOVE	LARRY	RECORD	TWIN
BEARD	DROWNED	LAYERS	ROBERT	ULTRA
BOMB	FLINT	LAZY	RUFUS	WEIRD
BROWN	FLY	LJ	SANDS	WELFARE
BUPHEAD	FOUR	MAGIC	SAVIOR	WHIRLPOOL
BYRON	GOD	MITCHELL	SCARY	WINDOWS
CARP	GODZILLA	NAZIS	SHOE	YAK
CODY	ICEBOX	NOTEBOOK	SUMMER	
CONK	JOEY	OVEN	SWEDISH	

CROSSWORD - Watsons Go To Birmingham –1963

Across
1. Byron was sent to stay with Grandma ___.
5. Byron thought this was the reason for signing for food.
7. Nickname for the family car: ___ Bomber.
10. Byron killed and buried it.
13. Momma said she would burn Byron's.
16. Byron called where Kenny went The World Famous Watson Pet ___
18. Rufus did not mind being these when playing dinosaurs.
20. Kenny was teased because he had a ___ eye.
21. It was set off in the church.
22. Rufus's brother
23. Momma made the children dress in ___ of clothes in winter.
25. Dad put a ___ player in the car.
26. Byron's head after Mr. Watson's punishment.
27. Make of the family car

Down
2. Byron killed bird with ____ Creme
3. Kenny's song: Yakety ___
4. Dad said they were tickling God's ___ as they drove.
6. He stole Kenny's dinosaurs: ___ Jones
8. Kenny's friend picked on by other kids
9. Momma had a list of who sat by these each day.
11. Kenny said Birmingham was like one.
12. Family nickname: ___ Watsons
14. What Kenny brought out of the church
15. Byron was caught with these in the bathroom.
17. Momma called Michigan a giant ___.
19. State where Grandma Sands lived
21. Older brother who helped Kenny at the end of the story
22. Game Byron and Buphead played with Larry: Great ___ Escape
15124. Kenny's description of the Appalachian Mountains

CROSSWORD ANSWER KEY - Watsons Go To Birmingham –1963

							1 S	A	N	D	2 S		3 Y		4 B
											5 W	6 E	L	F	A	R	E
			7 B	8 R	9 O	W	N	10 D	O	V	E		J		K	A
11 O				U		I		12 W			D					R
V			13 F	I	N	G	E	R	S		14 I			15 M		D
E				U		D		I		16 H	O	S	17 P	I	T	A	L
18 N	19 A	Z	I	S		O		R		O			H		C		T
	L					W		D		E			E		C	
20 L	A	Z	Y			S						21 B	O	M	B		H
	B							22 C	O	D	Y			O		E
23 L	A	Y	E	R	S			A				R			X		S
	M							25 R	E	C	O	R	D			
26 B	A	L	D		A			P				N				
					R											
			27 P	L	Y	M	O	U	T	H						

Across
1. Byron was sent to stay with Grandma ___.
5. Byron thought this was the reason for signing for food.
7. Nickname for the family car: ___ Bomber.
10. Byron killed and buried it.
13. Momma said she would burn Byron's.
16. Byron called where Kenny went The World Famous Watson Pet ___
18. Rufus did not mind being these when playing dinosaurs.
20. Kenny was teased because he had a ___ eye.
21. It was set off in the church.
22. Rufus's brother
23. Momma made the children dress in ___ of clothes in winter.
25. Dad put a ___ player in the car.
26. Byron's head after Mr. Watson's punishment.
27. Make of the family car

Down
2. Byron killed bird with ____ Creme
3. Kenny's song: Yakety ___
4. Dad said they were tickling God's ___ as they drove.
6. He stole Kenny's dinosaurs: ___ Jones
8. Kenny's friend picked on by other kids
9. Momma had a list of who sat by these each day.
11. Kenny said Birmingham was like one.
12. Family nickname: ___ Watsons
14. What Kenny brought out of the church
15. Byron was caught with these in the bathroom.
17. Momma called Michigan a giant ___.
19. State where Grandma Sands lived
21. Older brother who helped Kenny at the end of the story
22. Game Byron and Buphead played with Larry: Great ___ Escape
24. Kenny's description of the Appalachian Mountains

MATCHING 1 - Watsons Go To Birmingham –1963

___ 1. MAGIC   A. Byron killed and buried it.
___ 2. FOUR   B. He stole Kenny's gloves: ___ Dunn
___ 3. ROBERT   C. Pinnacle of Western Civilization: ___ tree
___ 4. FLINT   D. Momma did not like to show these when smiling.
___ 5. PINE   E. Grandma's dear friend: Mr. ___
___ 6. JOEY   F. Momma said she would burn Byron's.
___ 7. CONK   G. There was one for Coloreds Only in Birmingham.
___ 8. SQUIRRELS   H. Byron's head after Mr. Watson's punishment.
___ 9. BATHROOM   I. Dad did not keep his with the rest of the family's.
___10. PLYMOUTH   J. Momma's song was Under the ___.
___11. KING   K. Shortest length of time Byron would be in Alabama
___12. TEETH   L. Byron & Kenny's little sister; she left the bombed church
___13. WINDOWS   M. Michigan city where Watsons lived
___14. DOVE   N. Rufus and Cody thought the ones in Flint were skinny.
___15. BALD   O. Kenny's favorite toys
___16. FINGERS   P. Momma had a list of who sat by these each day.
___17. SUMMER   Q. Kenny's nickname for Byron: ___ Wonder
___18. BOARDWALK   R. Number of girls killed in the church bombing
___19. TOOTHBRSH   S. Make of the family car
___20. DINOSAURS   T. Kenny was waiting for this power to make him feel better.
___21. HOSPITAL   U. Byron called where Kenny went The World Famous Watson Pet ___
___22. LARRY   V. Byron was caught with these in the bathroom.
___23. COUCH   W. Kenny hid behind it every day.
___24. LIPLESS   X. Kenny said Larry was ___ of School.
___25. MATCHES   Y. What Byron had done to his hair

MATCHING 1 ANSWER KEY - Watsons Go To Birmingham –1963

T - 1.	MAGIC	A. Byron killed and buried it.
R - 2.	FOUR	B. He stole Kenny's gloves: ___ Dunn
E - 3.	ROBERT	C. Pinnacle of Western Civilization: ___ tree
M - 4.	FLINT	D. Momma did not like to show these when smiling.
C - 5.	PINE	E. Grandma's dear friend: Mr. ___
L - 6.	JOEY	F. Momma said she would burn Byron's.
Y - 7.	CONK	G. There was one for Coloreds Only in Birmingham.
N - 8.	SQUIRRELS	H. Byron's head after Mr. Watson's punishment.
G - 9.	BATHROOM	I. Dad did not keep his with the rest of the family's.
S -10.	PLYMOUTH	J. Momma's song was Under the ___.
X -11.	KING	K. Shortest length of time Byron would be in Alabama
D -12.	TEETH	L. Byron & Kenny's little sister; she left the bombed church
P -13.	WINDOWS	M. Michigan city where Watsons lived
A -14.	DOVE	N. Rufus and Cody thought the ones in Flint were skinny.
H -15.	BALD	O. Kenny's favorite toys
F -16.	FINGERS	P. Momma had a list of who sat by these each day.
K -17.	SUMMER	Q. Kenny's nickname for Byron: ___ Wonder
J -18.	BOARDWALK	R. Number of girls killed in the church bombing
I -19.	TOOTHBRSH	S. Make of the family car
O -20.	DINOSAURS	T. Kenny was waiting for this power to make him feel better.
U -21.	HOSPITAL	U. Byron called where Kenny went The World Famous Watson Pet ___
B -22.	LARRY	V. Byron was caught with these in the bathroom.
W 23.	COUCH	W. Kenny hid behind it every day.
Q -24.	LIPLESS	X. Kenny said Larry was ___ of School.
V -25.	MATCHES	Y. What Byron had done to his hair

MATCHING 2 - Watsons Go To Birmingham –1963

___ 1. FINGERS   A. Rufus and Cody thought the ones in Flint were skinny.
___ 2. SANDS   B. Momma had a list of who sat by these each day.
___ 3. CHURCH   C. Kenny thought the meeting would be like King Kong and ___.
___ 4. MATCHES   D. Byron was sent to stay with Grandma ___.
___ 5. SHOE   E. Kenny got caught in one at the Landing.
___ 6. BEARD   F. There was one for Coloreds Only in Birmingham.
___ 7. BYRON   G. Momma said she would burn Byron's.
___ 8. HOSPITAL   H. What Kenny brought out of the church
___ 9. CONK   I. State where Grandma Sands lived
___10. BOARDWALK   J. Momma's song was Under the ___.
___11. APPALACHIAN   K. What Byron had done to his hair
___12. WHIRLPOOL   L. Kenny said Birmingham was like one.
___13. COLLIER   M. Kenny thought these mountains were scary.
___14. TOOTHBRSH   N. Older brother who helped Kenny at the end of the story
___15. WINDOWS   O. They were to stay away from ___'s Landing.
___16. LARRY   P. Dad said they were tickling God's ___ as they drove.
___17. LAYERS   Q. He stole Kenny's gloves: ___ Dunn
___18. GOD   R. One boy at the Landing did this.
___19. DROWNED   S. Kenny said Byron was ___ of School.
___20. GODZILLA   T. Site of Bombings
___21. SQUIRRELS   U. Byron was caught with these in the bathroom.
___22. ALABAMA   V. Byron's head after Mr. Watson's punishment.
___23. BALD   W. Byron called where Kenny went The World Famous Watson Pet ___
___24. OVEN   X. Momma made the children dress in ___ of clothes in winter.
___25. BATHROOM   Y. Dad did not keep his with the rest of the family's.

MACTHING 2 ANSWER KEY - Watsons Go To Birmingham –1963

G - 1.	FINGERS	A.	Rufus and Cody thought the ones in Flint were skinny.
D - 2.	SANDS	B.	Momma had a list of who sat by these each day.
T - 3.	CHURCH	C.	Kenny thought the meeting would be like King Kong and ___.
U - 4.	MATCHES	D.	Byron was sent to stay with Grandma ___.
H - 5.	SHOE	E.	Kenny got caught in one at the Landing.
P - 6.	BEARD	F.	There was one for Coloreds Only in Birmingham.
N - 7.	BYRON	G.	Momma said she would burn Byron's.
W 8.	HOSPITAL	H.	What Kenny brought out of the church
K - 9.	CONK	I.	State where Grandma Sands lived
J - 10.	BOARDWALK	J.	Momma's song was Under the ___.
M ·11.	APPALACHIAN	K.	What Byron had done to his hair
E -12.	WHIRLPOOL	L.	Kenny said Birmingham was like one.
O -13.	COLLIER	M.	Kenny thought these mountains were scary.
Y -14.	TOOTHBRSH	N.	Older brother who helped Kenny at the end of the story
B -15.	WINDOWS	O.	They were to stay away from ___'s Landing.
Q -16.	LARRY	P.	Dad said they were tickling God's ___ as they drove.
X -17.	LAYERS	Q.	He stole Kenny's gloves: ___ Dunn
S -18.	GOD	R.	One boy at the Landing did this.
R -19.	DROWNED	S.	Kenny said Byron was ___ of School.
C -20.	GODZILLA	T.	Site of Bombings
A -21.	SQUIRRELS	U.	Byron was caught with these in the bathroom.
I - 22.	ALABAMA	V.	Byron's head after Mr. Watson's punishment.
V -23.	BALD	W.	Byron called where Kenny went The World Famous Watson Pet ___
L -24.	OVEN	X.	Momma made the children dress in ___ of clothes in winter.
F -25.	BATHROOM	Y.	Dad did not keep his with the rest of the family's.

JUGGLE LETTERS - Watsons Go To Birmingham –1963

1. KAY = 1. _____
Kenny's song: Yakety ___

2. NSSAD = 2. _____
Byron was sent to stay with Grandma ___.

3. ENKOTBOO = 3. _____
Where Momma kept the details of the trip

4. COIEXB = 4. _____
Momma called Michigan a giant ___.

5. IKNG = 5. _____
Kenny said Larry was ____ of School.

6. RCHCUH = 6. _____
Site of Bombings

7. HANPAAILPAC = 7. _____
Kenny thought these mountains were scary.

8. JL = 8. _____
He stole Kenny's dinosaurs: __ Jones

9. OWDSWNI = 9. _____
Momma had a list of who sat by these each day.

10. LAKROBADW =10. _____
Momma's song was Under the ___.

11. UVJELNIE =11. _____
Byron was officially called this since he turned thirteen.

12. NCKO =12. _____
What Byron had done to his hair

13. ELFEARW =13. _____
Byron thought this was the reason for signing for food.

14. SPELILS =14. _____
Kenny's nickname for Byron: ___ Wonder

15. SAEYRL =15. _____
Momma made the children dress in ___ of clothes in winter.

16. WESSDIH =16. _____
Byron killed bird with ____ Creme

17. ORRTEB =17. _____
Grandma's dear friend: Mr. ___

18. OOABMTRH =18. _____
There was one for Coloreds Only in Birmingham.

19. GRAMHNIIMB =19. _____
City where Momma originally came from.

20. BNOYR =20. _____
Older brother who helped Kenny at the end of the story

21. PRAC =21. _____
Game Byron and Buphead played with Larry: Great ___ Escape

22. LYF =22. _____
Dad whistled this tune: Straighten Up and ___ Right

23. LRLCEIO =23. _____
They were to stay away from ___'s Landing.

24. OGD =24. _____
Kenny said Byron was ___ of School.

25. OSEH =25. _____
What Kenny brought out of the church

JUGGLE LETTERS ANSWER KEY - Watsons Go To Birmingham –1963

1. KAY = 1. YAK
Kenny's song: Yakety ___

2. NSSAD = 2. SANDS
Byron was sent to stay with Grandma ___.

3. ENKOTBOO = 3. NOTEBOOK
Where Momma kept the details of the trip

4. COIEXB = 4. ICEBOX
Momma called Michigan a giant ___.

5. IKNG = 5. KING
Kenny said Larry was ___ of School.

6. RCHCUH = 6. CHURCH
Site of Bombings

7. HANPAAILPAC = 7. APPALACHIAN
Kenny thought these mountains were scary.

8. JL = 8. LJ
He stole Kenny's dinosaurs: ___ Jones

9. OWDSWNI = 9. WINDOWS
Momma had a list of who sat by these each day.

10. LAKROBADW = 10. BOARDWALK
Momma's song was Under the ___.

11. UVJELNIE = 11. JUVENILE
Byron was officially called this since he turned thirteen.

12. NCKO = 12. CONK
What Byron had done to his hair

13. ELFEARW = 13. WELFARE
Byron thought this was the reason for signing for food.

14. SPELILS = 14. LIPLESS
Kenny's nickname for Byron: ___ Wonder

15. SAEYRL = 15. LAYERS
Momma made the children dress in ___ of clothes in winter.

16. WESSDIH =16. SWEDISH
Byron killed bird with ____ Creme

17. ORRTEB =17. ROBERT
Grandma's dear friend: Mr. ___

18. OOABMTRH =18. BATHROOM
There was one for Coloreds Only in Birmingham.

19. GRAMHNIIMB =19. BIRMINGHAM
City where Momma originally came from.

20. BNOYR =20. BYRON
Older brother who helped Kenny at the end of the story

21. PRAC =21. CARP
Game Byron and Buphead played with Larry: Great ___ Escape

22. LYF =22. FLY
Dad whistled this tune: Straighten Up and ___ Right

23. LRLCEIO =23. COLLIER
They were to stay away from ___'s Landing.

24. OGD =24. GOD
Kenny said Byron was ___ of School.

25. OSEH =25. SHOE
What Kenny brought out of the church

VOCABULARY RESOURCE MATERIALS

VOCABULARY WORD SEARCH - Watsons Go To Birmingham –1963

```
E T A M I T L U H I L A R I O U S E W R
M K R U G G N I L B M U M B T L O L E W
U F Q G N D W C A L E S F P O O B E L K
L F P S A N S A T V F K G S L O B C F Q
A Y M Z S I N T I M I D A T E P Y T A N
T T Z J H B I J V L E N G F R L O R R N
E L C Q I B T Z Y V I K T W A R D O E E
E S U R N L C K I T N N D H T I H C R P
R T R G G E H V A G U O G U E H X U A T
H A V H S K R T N T H C R E D W T T B B
Y G E X K U I C S G J E N V N A H E I V
P G B H S O D N U O B L D G M E S D E Z
N E A O N C E D R O W S Y G T E R V S H
O R L S D Y H C R O S Q W I N P C A R K
T E L T V V C M C Q Y X C I B D C O T I
I D S I D Z U S U T G K O M L A T J N E
Z C P L V Y O A S F N R U R R I D F W G
E A V E S D R O P P I N G P A C E U E T
D C C T O E C X Y T T Q X R V C V R L N
T H U G S N Z H Y X S V T S T I L L S L
```

BOUND	HILARIOUS	PEON	SURVIVED
CARP	HOSTILE	RABIES	THUGS
CONK	HYPNOTIZED	SANITATION	TOLERATE
CROUCHED	INFECT	SCOWL	TORTURE
CURVEBALLS	INTIMIDATE	SENIORITY	TRAITOR
DAZZLE	JIVE	SLEW	ULTIMATE
DROWSY	MATURE	SNITCH	VITAL
DULL	MUGS	SOBBY	WAILING
EAVESDROPPING	MUMBLING	SQUARE	WELFARE
ELECTROCUTED	NIBBLE	STAGGERED	WHIRLPOOL
EMULATE	NUMB	STILL	WILIER
GENERATE	PACE	STINGY	
GNASHING	PATHETIC	STUNT	

VOCABULARY WORD SEARCH ANSWER KEY - Watsons Go To Birmingham –1963

```
E T A M I T L U H I L A R I O U S E W
M   U G G N I L B M U M     T L O   E
U   G N D W A   E           O O B   L
L   S   N S A T V         S L O B   F
A   Z   S I N T I M I D A T E P Y T A
T   Z   H B I J V L E N     R L O R R
E L C   I B T   V I K T     A R O   E
E S U   N L C   I T N       T I C R P
  T R   G E H V A   U O G U E H U   A
H A V       R T T   C R E   N A W T B
Y G E       U I S   E       N H E I
P G B H S O D N U O B L   M E S D   S
N E A O N   E D R O W S Y T E R     E
O R L S     H   O S   W I N     A   R
T E L T     C   C Q Y   C I B   C O T I
I D S I     U S   G   O M L A T N   E
Z   P L     O A   N R U   R I D F W
E A V E S D R O P P I N G P A C E U E
D       O E C       T       R   C R L
T H U G S   N       Y       S T I L L S L
```

BOUND	HILARIOUS	PEON	SURVIVED
CARP	HOSTILE	RABIES	THUGS
CONK	HYPNOTIZED	SANITATION	TOLERATE
CROUCHED	INFECT	SCOWL	TORTURE
CURVEBALLS	INTIMIDATE	SENIORITY	TRAITOR
DAZZLE	JIVE	SLEW	ULTIMATE
DROWSY	MATURE	SNITCH	VITAL
DULL	MUGS	SOBBY	WAILING
EAVESDROPPING	MUMBLING	SQUARE	WELFARE
ELECTROCUTED	NIBBLE	STAGGERED	WHIRLPOOL
EMULATE	NUMB	STILL	WILIER
GENERATE	PACE	STINGY	
GNASHING	PATHETIC	STUNT	

VOCABULARY CROSSWORD - Watsons Go To Birmingham –1963

Across
- 2. Not able to do something
- 5. Obligated or certain to do something
- 7. Faces
- 9. Disease of warm-blooded animals
- 11. Not able to feel emotions
- 14. Aid in the form of money and other benefits
- 15. Speed
- 16. Gangsters; violent criminals
- 18. Jazz or swing music
- 22. Having no motion
- 23. Give a disease to
- 26. Breed of large fish, including goldfish
- 27. To give pain or make another suffer
- 28. In a posture low to the ground

Down
- 1. A style that straightens curly hair
- 3. Take small, quick, playful bites
- 4. Try to be like someone else
- 6. Sleepy; tired
- 8. Produce or make
- 10. Stayed alive
- 12. Speaking unclearly in a low voice
- 13. Walked unsteadily
- 17. Highest quality
- 19. Put to death
- 20. Very low-paid worker
- 21. Stop; restrict
- 24. One who does something disloyal
- 25. More clever or deceiving

VOCABULARY CROSSWORD ANSWER KEY - Watsons Go To Birmingham –1963

	1			2	3					4			
	C			I	N	C	A	P	A	B	L	E	
5				6						7		8	
B	O	U	N	D		I				M	U	G	S
			9				10						
	N		R	A	B	I	E	S		U		E	
											11		12
	K		O		B		U			L	N	U	M	B
13			14						15				
S			W	E	L	F	A	R	E	P	A	C	E	U
16		17											
T	H	U	G	S		E		V			T		R	M
							18		19				
A		L		Y			J	I	V	E		E	A	B
				20		21					22		
G		T		P		S		V		X		S	T	I	L	L
		23								24				25
G		I	N	F	E	C	T		E		E	T	E	I	W
									26					
E		M		O		U		D		C	A	R	P	N	I
R		A		N		N				U		A		G	L
E		T				T				T		I			I
												27		
D		E						E		T	O	R	T	U	R	E
				28										
				C	R	O	U	C	H	E	D		O			R
													R			

Across
2. Not able to do something
5. Obligated or certain to do something
7. Faces
9. Disease of warm-blooded animals
11. Not able to feel emotions
14. Aid in the form of money and other benefits
15. Speed
16. Gangsters; violent criminals
18. Jazz or swing music
22. Having no motion
23. Give a disease to
26. Breed of large fish, including goldfish
27. To give pain or make another suffer
28. In a posture low to the ground

Down
1. A style that straightens curly hair
3. Take small, quick, playful bites
4. Try to be like someone else
6. Sleepy; tired
8. Produce or make
10. Stayed alive
12. Speaking unclearly in a low voice
13. Walked unsteadily
17. Highest quality
19. Put to death
20. Very low-paid worker
21. Stop; restrict
24. One who does something disloyal
25. More clever or deceiving

VOCABULARY MATCHING 1 - Watsons Go To Birmingham –1963

___ 1. STUNT   A. Not able to do something
___ 2. SENIORITY   B. Someone who tells on others
___ 3. CROUCHED   C. Full of tears; crying
___ 4. DULL   D. Amaze
___ 5. JIVE   E. Sense of right and wrong
___ 6. INCAPABLE   F. Breed of large fish, including goldfish
___ 7. SOBBY   G. Stayed alive
___ 8. WELFARE   H. Not generous; not willing to share
___ 9. INFECT   I. A style that straightens curly hair
___10. CARP   J. A large number
___11. SLEW   K. Not interesting; not exciting
___12. SNITCH   L. Related to mood or temperament
___13. SURVIVED   M. Put to death
___14. DAZZLE   N. Sad; causing feelings of pity
___15. MUMBLING   O. Stop; restrict
___16. STINGY   P. Aid in the form of money and other benefits
___17. DISPOSITION   Q. Having greater age or higher rank
___18. PATHETIC   R. Very funny
___19. CONK   S. Give a disease to
___20. MUGS   T. Speed
___21. CONSCIENCE   U. Faces
___22. EXECUTED   V. Jazz or swing music
___23. HILARIOUS   W. Speaking unclearly in a low voice
___24. BOUND   X. Obligated or certain to do something
___25. PACE   Y. In a posture low to the ground

VOCABURYARY MATCHING 1 ANSWER KEY - Watsons Go To Birmingham –1963

O - 1.	STUNT	A. Not able to do something
Q - 2.	SENIORITY	B. Someone who tells on others
Y - 3.	CROUCHED	C. Full of tears; crying
K - 4.	DULL	D. Amaze
V - 5.	JIVE	E. Sense of right and wrong
A - 6.	INCAPABLE	F. Breed of large fish, including goldfish
C - 7.	SOBBY	G. Stayed alive
P - 8.	WELFARE	H. Not generous; not willing to share
S - 9.	INFECT	I. A style that straightens curly hair
F - 10.	CARP	J. A large number
J - 11.	SLEW	K. Not interesting; not exciting
B - 12.	SNITCH	L. Related to mood or temperament
G - 13.	SURVIVED	M. Put to death
D - 14.	DAZZLE	N. Sad; causing feelings of pity
W 15.	MUMBLING	O. Stop; restrict
H - 16.	STINGY	P. Aid in the form of money and other benefits
L - 17.	DISPOSITION	Q. Having greater age or higher rank
N - 18.	PATHETIC	R. Very funny
I - 19.	CONK	S. Give a disease to
U - 20.	MUGS	T. Speed
E - 21.	CONSCIENCE	U. Faces
M - 22.	EXECUTED	V. Jazz or swing music
R - 23.	HILARIOUS	W. Speaking unclearly in a low voice
X - 24.	BOUND	X. Obligated or certain to do something
T - 25.	PACE	Y. In a posture low to the ground

VOCABULARY MATCHING 2 - Watsons Go To Birmingham –1963

___ 1. EXECUTED   A. Distractions
___ 2. SQUARE   B. Speaking unclearly in a low voice
___ 3. CURVEBALLS   C. Put to death
___ 4. WHIRLPOOL   D. Sleepy; tired
___ 5. BOUND   E. Grown-up; adult
___ 6. MATURE   F. A spiraling current of water
___ 7. INCAPABLE   G. Gangsters; violent criminals
___ 8. AUTOMATICALLY   H. Died by electric shock
___ 9. SOBBY   I. Clenching; grinding
___ 10. DULL   J. Not able to feel emotions
___ 11. STUNT   K. Full of tears; crying
___ 12. INTIMIDATE   L. Very funny
___ 13. HILARIOUS   M. Not interesting; not exciting
___ 14. ELECTROCUTED   N. Jazz or swing music
___ 15. SCOWL   O. Not able to do something
___ 16. WELFARE   P. Aid in the form of money and other benefits
___ 17. GENERATE   Q. Obligated or certain to do something
___ 18. NUMB   R. Done without thought
___ 19. THUGS   S. Having no motion
___ 20. STILL   T. Stop; restrict
___ 21. JIVE   U. Produce or make
___ 22. GNASHING   V. Create a feeling of fear in someone
___ 23. EAVESDROPPING   W. Angry expression
___ 24. MUMBLING   X. Listening in when the speaker does not know it
___ 25. DROWSY   Y. Out of touch; old fashioned

VOCABULARY MATCHING 2 ANSWER KEY - Watsons Go To Birmingham –1963

C - 1. EXECUTED		A. Distractions
Y - 2. SQUARE		B. Speaking unclearly in a low voice
A - 3. CURVEBALLS		C. Put to death
F - 4. WHIRLPOOL		D. Sleepy; tired
Q - 5. BOUND		E. Grown-up; adult
E - 6. MATURE		F. A spiraling current of water
O - 7. INCAPABLE		G. Gangsters; violent criminals
R - 8. AUTOMATICALLY		H. Died by electric shock
K - 9. SOBBY		I. Clenching; grinding
M - 10. DULL		J. Not able to feel emotions
T - 11. STUNT		K. Full of tears; crying
V - 12. INTIMIDATE		L. Very funny
L - 13. HILARIOUS		M. Not interesting; not exciting
H - 14. ELECTROCUTED		N. Jazz or swing music
W - 15. SCOWL		O. Not able to do something
P - 16. WELFARE		P. Aid in the form of money and other benefits
U - 17. GENERATE		Q. Obligated or certain to do something
J - 18. NUMB		R. Done without thought
G - 19. THUGS		S. Having no motion
S - 20. STILL		T. Stop; restrict
N - 21. JIVE		U. Produce or make
I - 22. GNASHING		V. Create a feeling of fear in someone
X - 23. EAVESDROPPING		W. Angry expression
B - 24. MUMBLING		X. Listening in when the speaker does not know it
D - 25. DROWSY		Y. Out of touch; old fashioned

VOCABURLARY JUGGLE LETTER - Watsons Go To Birmingham –1963

1. NBUM = 1. _____
Not able to feel emotions

2. GIBANJREB = 2. _____
Talking very quickly

3. IDNEETREMD = 3. _____
Firm; strong-minded

4. TSILL = 4. _____
Having no motion

5. LAEBCAINP = 5. _____
Not able to do something

6. SIALHIOUR = 6. _____
Very funny

7. HILLWROOP = 7. _____
A spiraling current of water

8. RTAOELTE = 8. _____
Put up with

9. METEALU = 9. _____
Try to be like someone else

10. ITANSOINAT =10. _____
Related to health and cleanliness

11. LINBGUMM =11. _____
Speaking unclearly in a low voice

12. OSLWC =12. _____
Angry expression

13. AAZLAYDPHRH =13. _____
Randomly; not planned

14. IRLWIE =14. _____
More clever or deceiving

15. TINIOISOSDP =15. _____
Related to mood or temperament

16. REAWLEF =16. _____
Aid in the form of money and other benefits

17. ERISAB =17. _____
Disease of warm-blooded animals

18. SOWRYD =18. _____
Sleepy; tired

19. AELZZD =19. _____
Amaze

20. EPNO =20. _____
Very low-paid worker

21. WELS =21. _____
A large number

22. ZTOYNEHIDP =22. _____
Put into a trance or sleep-like condition

23. SSTIGSENRPA =23. _____
Going to a place without permission

24. IGNWILA =24. _____
Crying

25. RVCLEAUBSL =25. _____
Distractions

VOCABURLARY JUGGLE LETTER ANSWER KEY - Watsons Go To Birmingham –1963

1. NBUM = 1. NUMB
   Not able to feel emotions

2. GIBANJREB = 2. JABBERING
   Talking very quickly

3. IDNEETREMD = 3. DETERMINED
   Firm; strong-minded

4. TSILL = 4. STILL
   Having no motion

5. LAEBCAINP = 5. INCAPABLE
   Not able to do something

6. SIALHIOUR = 6. HILARIOUS
   Very funny

7. HILLWROOP = 7. WHIRLPOOL
   A spiraling current of water

8. RTAOELTE = 8. TOLERATE
   Put up with

9. METEALU = 9. EMULATE
   Try to be like someone else

10. ITANSOINAT =10. SANITATION
    Related to health and cleanliness

11. LINBGUMM =11. MUMBLING
    Speaking unclearly in a low voice

12. OSLWC =12. SCOWL
    Angry expression

13. AAZLAYDPHRH =13. HAPHAZARDLY
    Randomly; not planned

14. IRLWIE =14. WILIER
    More clever or deceiving

15. TINIOISOSDP =15. DISPOSITION
    Related to mood or temperament

16. REAWLEF =16. WELFARE
Aid in the form of money and other benefits

17. ERISAB =17. RABIES
Disease of warm-blooded animals

18. SOWRYD =18. DROWSY
Sleepy; tired

19. AELZZD =19. DAZZLE
Amaze

20. EPNO =20. PEON
Very low-paid worker

21. WELS =21. SLEW
A large number

22. ZTOYNEHIDP =22. HYPNOTIZED
Put into a trance or sleep-like condition

23. SSTIGSENRPA =23. TRESPASSING
Going to a place without permission

24. IGNWILA =24. WAILING
Crying

25. RVCLEAUBSL =25. CURVEBALLS
Distractions

www.ingramcontent.com/pod-product-compliance
Lightning Source LLC
LaVergne TN
LVHW081534060526
838200LV00048B/2080